BRIGHT NOTES

WAR AND PEACE
BY
LEO TOLSTOY

Intelligent Education

**INFLUENCE
PUBLISHERS**

Nashville, Tennessee

BRIGHT NOTES: War and Peace

www.BrightNotes.com

No part of this publication may be used or reproduced in any manner whatsoever without written permission, except in the case of brief quotations in critical articles and reviews. For permissions, contact Influence Publishers http://www.influencepublishers.com.

ISBN: 978-1-645423-08-9 (Paperback)
ISBN: 978-1-645423-09-6 (eBook)

Published in accordance with the U.S. Copyright Office Orphan Works and Mass Digitization report of the register of copyrights, June 2015.

Originally published by Monarch Press.
Austin Fowler, 1965
2019 Edition published by Influence Publishers.

Interior design by Lapiz Digital Services. Cover Design by Thinkpen Designs.

Printed in the United States of America.

Library of Congress Cataloging-in-Publication Data forthcoming.
Names: Intelligent Education
Title: BRIGHT NOTES: War and Peace
Subject: STU004000 STUDY AIDS / Book Notes

CONTENTS

INTRODUCTION TO LEO TOLSTOY

THE LIFE AND CAREER OF LEO TOLSTOY

Count Leo Nikolayevich Tolstoy was born on August 28, 1828, on his father's estate of Yasnaya Polyana, in the Province of Tula, Russia. The Tolstoys were a family of the old Russian nobility who served the Czars and ruled the Empire. He was a count who was raised in a large family in the best tradition of the nobility. He was orphaned by the time he was nine, and his education was taken over by an aunt. Tolstoy entered the University of Kazan in 1844, where he studied oriental languages and later law, but he left in 1847 without receiving a degree.

In his youth Tolstoy led the usual easy-going life of young men of his class - lighthearted and full of pleasure seeking. However, as his diary reveals, he was incapable of completely indulging himself in this kind of existence. He began at an early age to try to find a rational and moral justification of life - this quest remained the dominant force of his mind throughout his life and career.

In 1851, Tolstoy enlisted in the army as a volunteer and served until 1854, fighting guerrilla tribesmen in the Caucasus. Later, he served as an officer during the Crimean campaign, and was involved in the siege of Sevastopol. His Sevastopol Stories appeared while the siege was still on.

He began his literary career with stories of reminiscence: *Childhood* (1852), *Boyhood* (1854), and *Youth* (1856). These stories gained him his first fame and he was welcomed by the literary circles of Petersburg and Moscow. But Tolstoy was too much of an aristocrat to like these semi-Bohemian intelligentsia, whom he considered self-consciously plebian. In turn, they disliked his superior attitude. They could not appreciate the experimental value of his later works, so his association with the literary world was quite short-lived.

The years 1856–61 were divided between Petersburg, Moscow, Yasnaya, and foreign countries. His travels to Europe left him disgusted with the materialistic values of the bourgeois civilization. In 1859 he started a school for peasant children at Yasnaya and wrote a primer, graded reader, and arithmetic book, which had an enormous circulation. In 1860 he was profoundly affected by the death of his brother Nicholas (who appears as Nikolai in *Anna Karenina*). This was Tolstoy's first encounter with the inevitability of death.

In 1862, he married Sophie Andreyevna Behrs. Tolstoy married her when she was eighteen and he was thirty-four. He had known her as a child and at one point had been practically engaged to one of her sisters. She was the loveliest of the daughters of Dr. Behrs, a prominent and highly successful physician. Tolstoy had made a point of not marrying into his own social class, because he had lost respect for it after a dashing and dissolute youth as a wealthy Barine (baron). By the time of his marriage, Tolstoy was no longer living in the big mansion at Yasnaya Polyana, because a series of high escapades and various army posts had left him in debt. He had been forced to sell it for the value of the bricks and other building materials.

The "little" white house at Yasnaya Polyana where Tolstoy brought his wife the day after the wedding was soon too small for the growing family. (The Tolstoys had a total of thirteen children.) Tolstoy kept adding wings and extensions. Tolstoy had to send for an English governess eventually. This situation was difficult for the young mother, who did not know English. However, her fluency in other languages proved a boon. Yasnaya Polyana was a multilingual center. The senior Tolstoys, like many of the Russian nobility, spoke a great deal of French together, and they knew Russian and German as well. Besides the footmen, the coppersmith who made and repaired samovars, the cook and the cook's son, the stablemen, the grooms, the shepherds, the agents, and the laundress, there was the favorite Alexei, the writer's personal servant who had been with Tolstoy ever since he and his brother were orphaned.

In addition to the permanent residents, there was always a conglomeration of relatives on long visits. (We are reminded of Dolly's visits to Levin in *Anna Karenina*.) Visitors came frequently for special entertainments and amateur theatricals.

In the winter there were fancy dress balls which were less sophisticated than similar parties in St. Petersburg or Moscow. Regardless of the demands of his writing, there were periods when Tolstoy would sit down for three hours a day and play the piano. Other times he would steal time, and rescue the children from their studies to teach them to ride bareback. Summers, the family would take short trips on foot or in carts to bathing spots. At harvest time, Tolstoy would spend the whole day in the fields where he would take his place in the line of reapers. The other nobles of the area criticized him strongly for this. In *Anna Karenina* there are several scenes where Levin (Tolstoy) participates in the work of the farm. There are also hunting scenes. Tolstoy could not forego a chance to go bird hunting when an old friend, brother, or guest came down for a shoot.

Amid the flurry of activity with the estate and his growing family, Tolstoy created two gigantic literary masterpieces. The peculiarities of his art are most spectacularly revealed in *War and Peace*, the creation of which took seven years (1862–8). It is a historical novel on a grandiose scale, unfolding the panorama of European events between 1805 and 1814, giving a detailed picture of Napoleon's campaign in Russia in 1812.

Anna Karenina, a novel of family life and contemporary manners, began in 1873. The first installments appeared in 1875, and the publication of the novel was completed in 1877. *Anna Karenina* leads up to the moral and religious crisis that was to revolutionize Tolstoy's entire life. Before he began to write it, he had already been thinking about new artistic methods - abandoning the psychological and analytical manner of superfluous detail and discovering a simpler narrative style that could be applied not only to the sophisticated and corrupt educated classes, but to the undeveloped mind of the people. Tolstoy's writings after 1880 are divided by a deep cleft from all his earlier work. By 1880 his so-called "conversion" was complete. He was no longer interested in producing literature, but in conveying a moral and religious message. He now preached a primitive Christianity purged of ritual, church organization, and priesthood. The important thing was that men should love one another. *In My Confession* (1879), he described his personal "transformation," a kind of mystic fervor combined with a glorifying of work. In *What Is to Be Done?* (1884), he attacked the evils of money and the life of the leisured and professional classes. In *What is Art?* (1897), he denounced art for art's sake, attacked many of the world's greatest writers, and insisted on religion and social purpose as the test of all art. He rejected his own greatest works. But he continued to write fiction, *The Kreutzer Sonata* (1889), a study of jealousy and a diatribe against sexual education of young men and women, and

Resurrection (1899), a long novel which reflected his negative attitude toward society.

After his conversion, Tolstoy became increasingly identified with religious populism - union and communion with working people as the moral and religious solution to all problems. He became alienated from his wife and children, who considered him an eccentric mystic. He renounced his own class, turned vegetarian, reduced his material needs to a minimum, and even renounced his copyrights. This religious populism ran parallel to the revolutionary social populism of the radical intelligentsia in Russia, which led to the downfall of Czarism just seven years after his death. Tolstoy caught pneumonia and died at Ostapovo, an obscure railroad station, on November 20, 1910. He was buried at Yasnaya Polyana.

THE WRITING OF ANNA KARENINA

The novel was slow in its conception and even slower in being written. Tolstoy, not long after the publication of *War and Peace*, which put him in the limelight of world literature, had an idea to write a novel about a woman in high society who deceives her husband. But he soon discovered that being a well-known figure was time-consuming. His correspondence was great. He was still a wealthy count with an estate to manage. His old interest in education did not flag. Accordingly, it was three years later, in 1873, when he really started on *Anna Karenina*. Another three years passed, and in December, 1876, Tolstoy's wife wrote to her sister, "We are at last writing *Anna Karenina* as it should be written; that is without interruption. Full of energy, concentrated, Lyovochka (the endearing diminutive name for Leon, Leo, or Lev) adds a whole chapter each day while I recopy as fast as my fingers can write; at this present, while I am writing to you, the pages of my letter cover the pages of the chapter he wrote yesterday ... ."

One must smile at her writing "without interruption." This amazing couple had thirteen children by 1888. Sophie, who copied *War and Peace* several times and went through all the drafts of *Anna Karenina*, once wrote that she was either pregnant or nursing the entire time. Sergei, Tolstoy's oldest son, has given us a clear picture of life at Yasnaya Polyana during the time when his father was writing *Anna Karenina*. His book, *Tolstoy Remembered*, was not translated into English and published (London) until 1961, more than fifty years after the great writer had died. Sergei's record of their life at this time is an expansive kaleidoscope of people, making one appreciate the skill with which Tolstoy wove so many of them into his writing, particularly in *Anna Karenina*.

The hint of bitterness that was to dominate much of Tolstoy's later writing is beginning to be evident in *Anna Karenina*. In the same sense there are indications of Tolstoy's religious "conversion," which possibly brought him more fame than *War and Peace* and *Anna Karenina*. The last chapters of *Anna Karenina*, we must remember, were written much later than the first. Tolstoy, who was famous for his many corrections and revisions, always regretted that he had started to put the opening books of *Anna Karenina* into print before the end was written. To be sure, he had outlined it in full detail nearly a year in advance of his agreement with the Russian Herald for serial rights.

Life had done much to change the author's viewpoint between February 1870, when he spoke of writing about "a woman who is married in high society, but who ruins herself," and January 1875, when the first installment appeared. For one thing, a close neighbor, Anna Pirogova, committed suicide by throwing herself under a train in June, 1872. In mid-May, 1873 he put aside the draft to take time to visit Samara (the second estate he owned) where the suffering of the Bashkirs as a result of drought aroused his sympathy; he raised nearly two million rubles and provided over 750,000 pounds of wheat for their relief.

In that same year, in November, he lost the first of his infant children. (He was to lose two more in as many years after.) The death of the eighteen-month-old Peter had a very sobering effect on the course of his authorship. He wrote, "One may take consolation in the fact that if one had to choose one of us eight, this death is the easiest of all and for all to bear; but a heart, especially that of a mother, is a wonderful manifestation of the Divinity on earth, it does not reason, so my wife is much stricken."

His sorrow was converted into a drive to work. He worked with extreme intensity. When he went back to *Anna Karenina*, he little realized how much work there was ahead of him. As a result of his laborious productive effort, he slumped off as soon as the opening pages were in print. The reviewers were enthusiastic but he claimed he was disgusted and bored. Instead of a further work cure, he took the summer off and went to Samara where he not only bought horses, but, to the delight of the Bashkirs, organized horse races. Sometimes a thousand tribesmen watched a single race.

Back home in the fall, his wife became gravely ill, giving birth prematurely to a little girl who lived only long enough to be christened. The next month, the old aunt who had brought him up died. Her death had the effect of regarding Tolstoy's evolution towards faith. The old lady had gone to her death, fearing and fighting it. To the end she maintained a lack of humility and insubordination to the will of God. Undoubtedly this attitude of hers affected Tolstoy's account of Nikolai's death. In February 1876, after the beginning, but before the completion of *Anna Karenina*, Tolstoy wrote; "I do not believe in anything that religion teaches us to believe in; yet at the same time I not only hate and scorn unbelief, I cannot see any possibility of living without faith, much less dying without one. So I am gradually building up my beliefs but they are all, even if firm, still very indefinite, lacking in distinctness and the capacity for consolation."

A month before this, he had written to his brother: "Nothing is left in life but to die. I feel this constantly." This reminds us of the scene where Levin speaks of "hiding the rope."

Although *My Confession* was not published until 1879, it is unquestionable that Tolstoy was going through a religious evolution during the writing of *Anna Karenina*. Because Tolstoy asks, through the mouths of so many characters, the eternal questions of all ages, the popularity of *Anna Karenina* continues.

TOLSTOY THE EDUCATOR

In addition to his educational work with peasants mentioned earlier, Tolstoy also spent a great deal of time on his children's education. He read to them regularly. He taught them mathematics, for which he devised a new method of multiplying. This system is similar to the contemporary "new math," now popularly called the "base five" concept. Instruction in the languages became the mother's province. Later, a German tutor was hired for the boys. Even so, Tolstoy took a hand especially when they participated in local exams. At one time he learned Greek to help his oldest son but became so interested in the Greek way of life that he altered many of his own viewpoints. These alterations are reflected in *Anna Karenina*.

While working on *Anna Karenina*, Tolstoy went ahead with the educational book, *The Alphabet*. He had tried setting up a school for the peasants at Yasnaya Polyana. He experimented with the Lancaster method. One winter his older children were entrusted with the education of the peasant children, who came to the house where they crowded the rooms and halls. Regardless of the shrieks and laughter the experiment was considered successful. In 1862, he published a pedagogical magazine, *Yasnaya Polyana*, in which he shocked his readers by contending that it was not intellectuals who should teach peasants, but vice versa.

TOLSTOY AND THE PEASANTS

From his childhood until his death, Tolstoy always saw agricultural work as man's means of providing all his needs. The **theme** of work is dominant in Tolstoy, particularly in *Anna Karenina*. Because of the influence of German medicine in Russia, Tolstoy took up the name Arbeitskur (Labor Cure). He felt that physical exercise insured a healthy body and a healthy mind. Tolstoy himself enjoyed good health. Even when he was "sick" after a long winter of indoor study, writing, and waiting on ailing children and a tire-out wife, he took a Kumiss cure by going down to Samara for a "rest" - "Rest" meant horseback riding, sleeping outdoors, examining property and digging for ancient ruins!

Tolstoy had, like most naturally healthy people, little patience with sickness. His own brother's sickness and death are mirrored in the harrowing account of Levin's brother, Nikolai. Tolstoy's evolution from a fear of death to an acceptance of death as a fact of life, even as an adventure not necessarily to be shunned, represents a major part of the fabric of *Anna Karenina*.

Tolstoy always admired the peasant's simple confrontations with life and death.

At one time Tolstoy tried to free the serfs. As a young intellectual he had always believed that slavery was immoral, that the salvation of the Russian economy rested on an agriculture maintained by free labor, and that only through education could the serf learn responsibility. As the landowner, Tolstoy went to a great deal of trouble in his attempt to get the serfs to accept their freedom. He made various arrangements by which they could obtain land through token payments of a few rubles each year over an extended period. The peasants, however, were suspicious and refused. They loved him as a man, but not as a member of his class. **Irony** lies in the fact that, intellectually, Tolstoy was an anarchist. Believing in the complete absence of government, he contended that government by its very nature engendered corruption. An official could not avoid dishonesty. Late in life Tolstoy gave away all his property.

TOLSTOY AS INNOVATOR

Tolstoy's enthusiasm for life is infectious. All the characters and their activities in *Anna Karenina* are interesting. The author's genius makes not only the extraordinary but the commonplace meaningful. The most complicated personality, even Anna herself, gains clarity when placed alongside a peasant who chews a wisp of hay at the roadside. Tolstoy was forever curious about the whole person, and the whole person was more than a list of personality traits an author might jot down. The heart often transcends reason. That mankind is weak, as well as strong, is a primary fact of life Tolstoy never forgot. His characters are revealed by two distinct methods.

In the first instance, his masses of characters are revealed in their relationships with each other. We see them at large dinner parties, at the opera in between the acts, at the races, in railroad stations, in military barracks. Their outward movements and their public and social faces tell tales about their inner souls. Opposed to this restless, yet formalized, motion picture of life, Tolstoy sets the still slide of a single individual. Here he is an innovator, along with other nineteenth century figures such as Balzac and Dostoevsky. For an author to climb inside his characters and do their soul searching was new to the novel. In a sense Tolstoy has his characters think out loud for the reader's benefit. Tolstoy was criticized for this. It was said that his people are too introspective. Their inner disputations disturb the flow of action in the story too frequently. These halts are indeed noticeable, in particular with the autobiographical character of Levin. On the other hand, the personality of Anna grows with her struggles and the personality of Count Vronsky, her lover, shrinks for the lack of them.

SUMMING UP

War and Peace, which was Tolstoy's gigantic novel that preceded *Anna Karenina*, established his reputation. It is usually accorded the distinction of being the best of Tolstoy. There are many who dispute this, preferring *Anna Karenina*. Some reasons are obvious. In the first place *Anna Karenina* is free of the long military passages in *War and Peace* that seem dull to many readers. In the second place it is contended that *War and Peace* holds itself in first place because it was first in time.

Immediately after *Anna Karenina*, Tolstoy experienced his so-called religious "conversion." The novels that followed this change revealed Tolstoy primarily as a humanist, philosopher and commentator on the contemporary scene, rather than as an artist. Because there was a hint of this "conversion" toward the end of *Anna Karenina*, there is an easy tendency to link it with the later books. On the other hand it should be remembered that the strength of *War and Peace*, which rests on the author's magnificent panorama of the Russian nobility and the people who lived on the fringes of such society, is redoubled in *Anna Karenina*. The marriages and the family life of the three women give the later novel a unity and artistic structure lacking in the first book. In addition, the fact that one of the marriages is a representation of the author's own lends support to its **realism** and enhances its interest.

It is to be remembered that Tolstoy wrote for his own class, aristocrats who read Dickens and Jane Austen, Flaubert and Gautier, Schiller and Goethe in the original languages. It is ironic that he did not write for the common man who is now his strongest admirer-so much so that new translations are continuously appearing in most languages. The books that have been written about Tolstoy fill many shelves on university libraries. So many books certainly represent a divergence of opinion. Fortunately for the book lover and poet, these tomes are more concerned with Tolstoy as a prophet, than as an artist. It must be admitted that as a prophet he is to be commended for his prediction of the Russian revolution. As a religious figure, he is also admired by many or his sense of pan-religionism, the Buddhistic views of Christianity which seem to be relevant to today's ecumenical perspectives.

A NOTE ON RUSSIAN NAMES

The title *Anna Karenina* sometimes becomes *Anna Karenin*. Anna's husband is Karenin. In Russian a is usually the feminine ending, but Karenin has become Karenina in translation. Accordingly, we have Mrs. or Madame Karenina. More usually she is called, Russian style, Anna Arkadyevna. This patronymic stems from her father's name, Arkady; thus she is Anna, daughter of Arkady. In the same sense, Anna's brother, Prince Oblonsky is called Stepan Arkadyevich. Fortunately the family nicknamed him Stiva. It is also comforting to the English reader that Oblonsky's wife, the Princess Darya Alexandrovna Shcherbatsky is called Dolly. The masculine suffixes ovich, ievich (or ich and ych) are similar to the English prefixes Mac or O'. Feminine endings include ovna, ievna, and ishna.

In this novel there are many, many characters with difficult names. However, they are so clearly drawn, and they appear in the story so frequently that one has little trouble keeping them straight. Even at the opening the new names do not flood the pages, but are introduced in orderly sequence. By the end of part one, roughly page 125, each is an old friend, or enemy.

WAR AND PEACE

· ·

Leo Tolstoy's major work, *War and Peace*, is surely one of the most exciting novels ever written. It is also one of the greatest masterpieces of world literature. Yet it is one of those books which more people read about than actually read.

REASONS FOR GREATNESS

There are reasons for this. It is a very long novel, over 1600 pages, as thick with experience and dense with characters and settings as life itself. It is, in fact, a whole new world. The reader may be somewhat overawed by its length, its bulk, and this may deter him from one of literature's most rewarding experiences. My job, as I see it, is to map this world for you to guide you through its streets and houses and country roads, and to introduce you to its emperors and generals, aristocrats and peasants, its lovely women and ancient crones. You will visit army camps and the salons of the Czar. You will meet one of literature's most fascinating women, the delightful Natasha, share the joy and pain of the discovery of life's meaning with Pierre, and live the adventures of the enigmatic Prince Andrew. But these are only a few of the many rich experiences awaiting you in Tolstoy's epic novel.

THE WORLD OF WAR AND PEACE

When Tolstoy chose the title *War and Peace* for this great work, he did not do so idly. Tolstoy wishes to show, once for all, not merely the glory of **epic** struggle, but also the horror of man to man combat; not only the loveliness of peace, but also, for some, its boredom. Gradually, leisurely, Tolstoy creates the imposing edifice which is his world of peace. It is a solid world, so solid that the reader knows it as well, if not better than, the world in which he exists. Here, Tolstoy's incredible and seemingly simple ability to make us believe in the reality of his settings and characters is demonstrated, moment by moment, sentence by sentence. Then, having established this world for us in all its dimensions, slowly, inexorably the great waves of war advance upon it, first dimly and from a great distance, then more closely until the tides of battle swirl in the very heart of Moscow itself, rocking Tolstoy's world to its very foundations. Here, in a work full of climaxes, is the great climax. An old and well-rooted society must fight for its very survival. We witness the agony and grandeur of battle, the clash of will against will, the depths of human endurance and the will to survive. We know, because we have become part of this world, that it will never be the same again. We know, too, the horror and destruction of war, its senseless and monstrous waste of all those things which human beings value and cherish.

NO MORALIZING

Yet Tolstoy refuses to moralize, for that is the lazy way and Tolstoy is never lazy. He concentrates on human beings, what they do, how they look, what they say. In no other novel are you so completely "there." Because you are there, you, as in life itself, must make your own evaluations about people and events. Tolstoy never sentimentalizes or distorts by cutting out cardboard figures, so to speak, and naming them. He knows that persons essentially good sometimes do selfish and stupid things, that egotists may sometimes have good reasons for being egotistical, that a pretty butterfly of a girl can be as capable of heroic self-denial as a saint. He knows that a society dandy can be as troubled about the meaning of life, about God and immortality, as anyone else.

THE READER'S REWARD

Reading him, the reader is forced to stretch his moral and ethical muscles; he is forced to grow up. Tolstoy allows a reader to do steadily and for a long time what most of us rarely do at all- withhold judgment, see people and events in the round, in all their dimensions, not as they ought to be but as they are. Reading *War and Peace* is truly an education in itself. It is for this reason that *War and Peace* is indispensable. It offers us not one but many love stories, adventures without parallel for excitement and tension, **episodes** so varied and gripping that you will be unable to put the book down. Death scenes and love scenes, hunting scenes and war scenes unfold with almost unbelievable fertility before us. In the end, however, the importance of *War and Peace* is that is matures one. Very few men have been able to behold so much of the visible universe so steadily and without distortion. Even fewer men have been capable of making their vision perceptible to others. Tolstoy was one of them.

BIOGRAPHICAL INTRODUCTION

The man who was able to imagine and construct the world of *War and Peace* was no ordinary man. In some ways he was the most extraordinary man who ever lived. His life was long and varied in its experience. One point the reader may well keep in mind, however, is that in all his work Tolstoy made consistent use of the facts of his own life. He has been called the most autobiographical of all major novelists. It is the absolute validity of his vital intellectual, spiritual, and physical existence that keeps Tolstoy from ever being merely fanciful.

BIRTH AND ANCESTRY

Count Leo Nikolayevich Tolstoy was born August 28, 1828, into a family of the old Russian aristocracy. The family traced its ancestry to one Indris, who in 1353 came to Russia from the West "with two sons and three thousand retainers." Because of the centuries-old custom of intermarriage among the aristocratic class, Tolstoy could claim kinship with nearly every family of any social consequence throughout Russia. In this thoroughly class-structured society Tolstoy was born near the top of what can be pictured as a huge pyramid with the Emperor (Czar) at the isolated tip and the first families just below, followed by the various strata of the lesser gentry, bureaucrats, functionaries, and town dwellers down to the innumerable masses of peasants and serfs. One of the facts about a pyramid is that the stones at the base not only support the top stones, but also are most crushed by them. Not the least extraordinary thing about Tolstoy's life was that although born, so to speak, just under the capstone, he ended it, by his own choice, at the bottom of his society, on a level with his beloved peasants.

TOLSTOY'S FAMILY

Tolstoy was born on the family estate called Yasnaya Polyana ("clear fields" of "glades"), some hundred and thirty miles south of Moscow. Here with his three older brothers, mother, father, numerous female relatives, servants, and serfs he lived as he himself wrote in his first published work, *Childhood*, "an enviable and idyllic existence." Tolstoy's father, Nikolai, had been in the army during Napoleon's invasion of Russia. He was captured by the French and was not released until the Russians entered the French capital in March, 1814. This kindly, energetic man, who was the model for Nikolai Rostov in *War and Peace*, was a good father to his four sons. He had married the wealthy, if not beautiful, Princess Marya Volkonsky in 1822, thus acquiring Yasnaya Polyana. She was a brilliant and well-educated woman whose intellectual abilities were inherited by all her children. Her profound moral and spiritual qualities, however, went to Leo, for whom they unlocked the only truths about human existence which he would ultimately regard as important.

THE ORPHAN

Unfortunately this rare woman died when Leo was only two years old. He was then raised by his paternal grandmother, Pelayeya, who lived with them, and by two aunts; Alexandra, who had been married to a mad Baltic count, and Tatyana, whom his father had once loved. They lived together in an atmosphere of such intense familiar warmth and affection that it permeated the entire atmosphere of his existence. It was impossible that when his childhood was over he would ever find such love again. Tolstoy's life-long search for the simple love and happiness of his childhood is another fact which we must keep in mind in reading *War and Peace*.

In 1837, the Tolstoy family went to Moscow to live. For the first time young Leo realized that not everyone loved him. Certain elements were introduced into his existence which disturbed him, and so extraordinary was his sensibility that each of these disturbances became life-long influences. His new tutor, a Frenchman of elegance, threatened to whip him; an indignant groundskeeper turned him and his brothers out of a lovely garden. From these experiences sprang his lifelong hatred of artificiality, violence of any kind, and authoritarianism. Then within a year his father and grandmother died, leaving the children orphans. Aunt Alexandra became their legal guardian. He continued to lead the wealthy, sheltered life of the aristocracy. Little Leo fell in love. Sonya Koloskin was to remain all his life, like Dante's Beatrice, the ideal of chaste love. In 1841, Aunt Alexandra died. The boys were taken to Kazan to live with another aunt, Pelayeya Greshkov.

LIFE IN KAZAN

Here in Kazan, Leo, never a good student, after first failing to pass the matriculation examination, subsequently passed and was admitted to the University in 1844. He originally entered the school of Oriental languages. Later he entered the school of Law. However, he was much more interested in enjoying to the fullest what benefits student status offered. Living with his older brothers, with a carriage of his own and a personal servant, he gave himself up to the dissolute life which was regarded as not only natural but desirable for the young aristocrats of the time. Tolstoy was torn by two contrary desires: to live to the full the life offered him and at the same time, to deny its materialistic values, its disregard of the spirit, its artificiality, its ignorance of all those values of the spirit and mind which he valued most. On the one hand, he became utterly committed to its habit of valuing everyone according to his wealthy and family background; he actually kept lists of his acquaintances weighed in precisely this way. On the other hand, his disgust with himself for doing this became deeper and deeper. He kept lists also, of his failures to remind himself how short of his ideals he fell. The self-analysis he practiced in his diary neither falsified nor omitted anything. This developed his already acute eye for the roots of human action and motives. He observed and recorded everything, remembering the casual gesture, the look in an eye, the tone of a voice which betrayed character.

FOR THE NEXT TWENTY YEARS

For the Next Twenty Years, from the time he became a student and entered society at fourteen, until he was thirty-four and married, he was to struggle against the strong appetites of his sensual nature. During these years he was to leave the university, join his brother's regiment among the Cossacks, see fighting on the Caucasus, be decorated for bravery more than once, fight at Sevastopol in the Crimean War, write, publish his first books, notably *Childhood* and *Sevastopol Sketches*, return to carry out advanced educational experiments among his serfs at Yasnaya Polyana, throw himself into the work of reform, suffer a spiritual crisis as does Pierre in *War and Peace*, and finally marry. Thereafter he lived a happy and productive life on his estate. It was during this final period, beginning in 1863 and for the next seven years, that he wrote *War and Peace*. It will be seen how the novel draws together all those interests which had occupied him in his life up to then.

CONVERSION, QUEST, AND DEATH

The creation of *War and Peace* is by no means the last important event in Tolstoy's life. He went on to write other literary masterpieces, notably the great *Anna Karenina*. However, family happiness, worldly success, the esteem in which he was beginning to be held throughout the world only served to torment him. He had all that life had to offer, and he found it empty, tasteless. He had to know the ultimate truths. Horrified by the absolute meaninglessness of existence he came to the verge of suicide. He kept asking, "What for? Where does it all lead?" We are reminded of both Pierre and Prince Andrew here. Now, with renewed force, at the age of fifty he was pressed to the edge of self-destruction by the simple question; "Given death, what is life's meaning?" All this he documents in his beautiful book, Confession. He explored all the possible answers offered by science and found them wanting. He investigated both Eastern and Western religions. He had long since given up his faith in the tenets of Russian Orthodoxy. Now he demanded to know that "something by which people live." His struggle was long and intense. Led by the simple faith of the peasants, he came at last to believe that religion, in spite of practice and rituals which he could not accept, contained the only explanation of life's meaning. Love of God and men, service, the sufferance of violence, dedication to humanity - these were the tenets of his final faith. He had achieved wealth, fame, artistic success of the highest order; now he dedicated his life to moral perfection. During the rest of his life he was true to his decision, giving up, in so far as he could, all his worldly wealth to the peasants, living as a peasant, and being, as one might expect, a scandal to all those who did not understand.

In the end, prompted by the desire to retire entirely from the world to give himself up to contemplation of the mysteries of love and God "in peace and solitude," he started on a journey to travel like a holy man until death came upon him. But his long cherished wish was not to be fulfilled, at least not as he expected. Death was to come sooner than he could have realized, for he was on his way to death. On the railroad journey he caught a chill. A fever developed. At the Astapovo railroad station (now called the Leo Tolstoy station) he was put to bed in the stationmaster's tiny house where, on Nov. 1, 1910, he died. His last words, according to his daughter, Dushan, who had accompanied him on his last journey were, "Truth ... I love much." He was 82 years old.

INTRODUCTION TO WAR AND PEACE

The publishing history of *War and Peace* is very complicated. The text the reader uses is one translated from the 1886 edition in four volumes. The Simon and Schuster edition (the one most frequently available to the student and the one which I will use), in a translation by Louise and Alymer Maude, runs to some 1600 pages, in 15 parts, each part having many chapters. Other translations run to over 1500 pages. It is the longest nineteenth-century Russian novel; indeed it is one of the longest novels in any language in any century. For it Tolstoy devoured whole libraries, created over five hundred characters, of whom only one hundred can be called major. Besides these, there are whole armies, mobs, crowds, and even distinctly memorable animals, especially hunting dogs and, not least, a most amazing wolf.

WAR AND PEACE AS HISTORY

It is an historical novel in two senses: one, because it deals with a particular and real segment of human history, i.e., Russia before, during, and after invasion by Napoleon; and two, because it is, among other things, Tolstoy's analysis and demonstration of what he believes history should be and how it should be written. Briefly, he was committed to the idea that it is not individuals (heroes) who control the mechanics of human destiny, but "the ferment of the people." In this sense, War and Peace is a vast panorama depicting this "ferment of the people" poked into activity by the flaming lance of war. From time to time, notably in the last section, Tolstoy pauses to write what appear to be essays on the nature of history. The best way to read these segments is as part and parcel of the Tolstoyean world; they do not necessarily have much validity outside the novel. One critic suggests that these elements operate in the novel in much the same way Homer's or Milton's theology operates in their epics, the Odyssey and Paradise Lost.

WAR AND PEACE AS EPIC

This brings us to the next important thing to know about War and Peace. It is an **epic**. Although historical, it is historical in the same way as, say, Homer's Odyssey. A true **epic** deals with all of reality, or as much as is held valuable in a culture. It tends to be encyclopedic; it attempts to deal with the ultimate conditions of human existence; it hopes to create archetypes and models of value to a culture. A national **epic** attempts to unify a people by isolating the identity of that people, its peculiar and specific character, from all the other peoples of the earth. In this sense, *War and Peace* is not only an **epic**, but the national epic of the Russian people. By concentrating on the years in their history when for the first time all Russia's various peoples, of different ethnic and linguistic traditions, united to repel a common enemy, Tolstoy shows the birth of Russia as a nation. He was not alone in his belief that "Holy Russia" has a special destiny to save the world. This idea, in part, was involved with rejection of the West and its materialistic culture. How better to dramatize this conflict of values than by showing the salvation of Russia by the Russian people, led by the wily folk, the peasant-like Kutusov, who in *War and Peace* destroys Napoleon. This is the **epic** struggle and one of the great unifying **themes** of the book.

WAR AND PEACE AS NOVEL

But *War and Peace* is also a novel. Tolstoy for many years could not quite decide what precisely he was writing, an **epic**, a poem, a story, a chronicle. Finally, he called it a novel. And certainly it is a novel, which may be defined as a narrative providing the reader with individual experience as against the **epic** which provides the reader with communal values, the experience of the people. It is in this sense that *War and Peace* is a novel which tells the story of three families, the Rostovs, the Bolkonskys and the Bezukhovs. Generally speaking, the Rostovs are modeled on the Tolstoys, that is, his father and his family; the Bolkonskys on the Volkonskys, his mother's people. Prince Andrew and Pierre are both projections of Tolstoy's own personality. It is these two last named characters on whose stories I shall concentrate as providing the most easily available, consistent strand through *War and Peace*. They engage our hearts, they stand out against the slow and inexorable movements of destiny, for finally Tolstoy is not concerned with man in the mass nor truth in the abstract but with particular, specific individuals whose experiences he attempts to describe with accuracy. If there is "truth" in art, it is in such accuracy.

HISTORICAL BACKGROUND OF WAR AND PEACE

It is important for an understanding of Tolstoy's novel to have a general view of the events which lead up to it and those with which it deals. After the overthrow of the revolutionary French government in November 1799, Napoleon, who had been a general, quickly assumed control of France under the title of First Consul. In three years he had himself made chief ruler for life, and in two more years was made Emperor of the French. Ambitious for conquest to a superhuman degree, he had already solidified his control of Italy in two campaigns (1796–7 and 1800). He had repeatedly defeated Prussia and Austria, and these were happy to assuage their pride by the partition of Poland. Napoleon, for all intents and purposes, was master of Europe. But his ambition was not satisfied.

ENGLAND AND RUSSIA

There were only two directions in which Napoleon could go, East and West. The French emperor chose to go first for England. Allying himself with Spain, he prepared a great fleet for the invasion of England. This fleet, under Admiral Villeneuve, was destroyed by the great Englishman Nelson at the famous battle of Trafalgar in 1805. In 1804, a conspirator by the name of de Bourbon Conde, Duc d'Enghien was executed by Napoleon's order. It was mistakenly assumed in Russia that this nobleman was the rightful heir to the throne of France. (It is about this death that much of the talk in Anna Sherer's salon revolves in the first chapter of the novel.) The immediate result of this was that Tsar Alexander I of Russia withdrew his Ambassador from Paris; Napoleon, in retaliation, withdrew his from Petersburg. The situation became worse when Napoleon had himself crowned King of Italy in 1805. Alexander began negotiations with England for the purpose of forcing Napoleon to withdraw from Italy and guarantee the independence of Switzerland and Holland. Secret preparations went on to hold Napoleon. An alliance was formed among Russia, England, Sweden, Austria, Naples, and Prussia. War followed. It is the first campaign of this war which is the subject of most of Books One, Two, and Three. Fought in Austria, it culminated in the famous battle of Austerlitz in December, 1805. However, the war dragged on for another two years. In 1807, after the Battle of Friedland, a treaty of peace was signed. The Russian and French emperors formed an uneasy alliance which lasted five years.

THE CAMPAIGN OF 1812

Peace was not to last. Napoleon, as Hitler was to do more than a hundred years later, broke the treaty and marched on the East. It is of course this campaign which is the main historical event of the novel. Pushing on with his accustomed success, Napoleon quickly reached the city of Smolensk in August of 1812. Here the unexpected happened. The citizens, instead of merely accepting conquest as had the citizens of all the hundreds of cities Napoleon had previously invaded, burned the city and fled. Continuing on to Moscow, his goal, Napoleon was finally met by the Russian forces, under General Kutuzov, on September 7, 1812, at the horrifyingly bloody battle of Borodino. The battle was, in Tolstoy's opinion, won by the Russians, although they continued to retreat, by-passing Moscow to await the right moment to strike. Napoleon swept ahead and occupied the ancient city, but here too, as at Smolensk, the citizens had fled. The French occupied the empty city until October when Napoleon ordered an evacuation. Disordered, undisciplined, burdened by loot, the French were pursued by the now inflamed and fully strengthened Russian forces. The great Napoleonic force was harried and cut to pieces, and bit by bit destroyed. Acknowledging defeat, not by the Russian army as such, but by the complex of forces made up of that army, the Russian people themselves, weather, and a loss of purposeful goal, Napoleon abandoned his army to make its own way home in December. By December 18, he was in Paris. The Russian invasion had failed utterly.

IMPORTANT CHARACTERS IN WAR AND PEACE

Pierre, Count Bezukov, one of the two main male characters.

Andrew, Prince Bolkonsky, one of the two main male characters.

Natasha, Countess Rostova, the main female character.

Prince Nicholas Bolkonsky, Andrew's father.

Princess Mary Bolkonskaya, his daughter, Andrew's sister.

"Koko," Andrew's son by his first wife Lise.

Princess ELizabeth (Lise) Bolkonskaya, Andrew's wife.

Count Ilya Rostov, Natasha's father.

Count Nicholas Rostov, his elder son.

Countess Vera Rostova, Natasha's sister.

Sonya, niece of the Rostovs, Natasha's friend.

Prince Vasili Kuragin, a nobleman.

Princess Helene Kuragina, his daughter, Pierre's first wife.

Prince Hippolyte Kuragin, silly elder son of Vasili.

Prince Anatole Kuragin, Vasili's corrupt younger son.

Anna Pavlovna Sherer, Maid of Honor to the Empress, society hostess.

Princess Anna Drubetskya, Boris' mother, impoverished gentlewoman.

Marya Akhrosimova, the "terrible dragon" of Moscow society.

Princess Catiche, Pierre's cousin.

Mlle. Bourienne, Princess Mary Bolkonskaya's French companion.

Mary Hendrikhovna, wife of regimental doctor, Nicholas Rostov's friend.

Julie Karagina, heiress, confidante of Mary Bolkonsky.

Dolokhov, officer, gambler, reckless friend of Anatole Kuragin.

Alphonse Berg, Vera Rostova's husband.

Prince Boris Drubetsky, Natasha's childhood sweetheart.

Bilibin, Andrew's friend in diplomatic service.

Michael Kutuzov, commander-in-chief of Russian army.

Francis II, Emperor of Austria.

Alexander I, Tsar of Russia.

Napoleon Bonaparte, Emperor of France.

Peter Bagration, commander of Russian army.

Count Rostopchin, governor general of Moscow.

Captain Tushin, an army officer.

Platon Karataev, captured Russian peasant soldier.

WAR AND PEACE

BOOK ONE

....

CHAPTER ONE

It is July, 1805, in St. Petersburg (now Leningrad), Tsarist Russia. The book begins with the greeting Anna Sherer, Maid of Honor to the Dowager Empress Fedorovna, gives to Prince Kuragin, first guest at her soiree. Her first words refer to Napoleon, who, if anyone is, is the antagonist in the book. In the conversation which ensues, Prince Kuragin and Anna Sherer make oblique reference to numerous **themes** which will be developed later-war, Napoleon as an ogre, family relations, the God appointed task of Tsar Alexander I to save Europe and civilization. As other guests arrive, the focus shifts to various groupings. Pierre, one of the heroes of the story, arrives; he is fresh from his studies abroad and new to society. Later Prince Andrew, the other hero, arrives to escort home Lise, his pregnant wife of one year. Pierre disgraces himself by being natural and impetuous in his enthusiasms. An old and warm friendship, it is obvious, exists between Pierre and Andrew.

They agree to meet later at Andrew's home. The soiree comes to an end with the foolish Prince Hippolyte, Prince Kuragin's son, flirting with Princess Lise.

Comment

Tolstoy had the greatest difficulty, according to R. F. Christian, an authority on the manuscript's development, in deciding how to start. Having discarded a long introduction, he decided to follow ancient **epic** practice and plunge into the middle of things (in medias res). At first, because of this, the reader may feel lost: all the names and references without any elaborate explanation may confuse him. However, Tolstoy had his reasons. The most important of these is that he wished to introduce his characters obliquely, as one meets them in life. Notice how Pierre is introduced; he is "a stout, heavily built young man with close cropped hair, spectacles ... . Anna _____ greeted him with the nod she accorded to the lowest hierarchy in her drawing room ... a look of anxiety and fear" comes over her face "at the sight of something too large and unsuited to the place ..." Hardly an epic hero. The fact is, Pierre, though not without fault, is natural; he is not affected and artificial, and these are mandatory characteristics of conduct in Anna's drawing room. Having established for the reader the evolved and sophisticated nature of this society (notice Prince Kuragin again who says, automatically, things he does not even wish to be believed), Pierre's naturalism of behavior does appear rude. Prince Andrew, on the other hand, knows to perfection the role demanded of him in society. However, unlike Pierre, who is outside it, Andrew has seen through it. He is suffering acutely from boredom, ennui, because society has nothing more to offer him, and, as we shall see, he demands more of existence than the role society affords him. Tolstoy will sound these notes of artificiality, unnaturalness, and world weariness again and again. Culture, he will say, being materialistic and artificial, is evil. One may escape the evil only by naturalness, by simplicity, by repudiating all that this kind of world has to offer. Andrew, in fact, has already joined his uncle, General Kutuzov, as aide-de-camp. He is repudiating this life. Let me make two more points: First, Tolstoy's interest is not merely in what his characters do, but in why they do it. Here in this chapter alone numerous examples may be found. Let one suffice. After Pierre's embarrassing outbreak, the almost idiotic Prince Hippolyte tells a silly and pointless story. Anna appreciates his "social tact" in covering up the silence and we are left to understand that this is why the story was told. Tolstoy wishes us to see his characters in this round, neither completely good nor completely bad. Anna, a brittle figurine of a woman, suddenly displays "Christian mildness" in forgiving Pierre his indiscretion; Prince Andrew, with whom the reader is made to feel the greatest sympathy, is, however, rude to his wife; Pierre's absent-mindedness, amiable as it is, leads him to disregard ordinary human kindness in walking away from Anna's ancient aunt before that extremely dull woman has finished speaking.

CHAPTER TWO

The guests leave. Prince Andrew makes it known to the foolish foppish Prince Hippolyte that he despises him. In separate carriages Pierre and Andrew go to Andrew's new home-he is, after all, married but a year. Pierre, arriving first, takes a book from the library's shelves (it is Caesar's Commentaries) and throws himself down on a sofa. Andrew comes in and there is warm and friendly discussion. This Andrew, so different from the one the reader has met at the soiree, is, we understand, closer to the genuine Andrew. Andrew urges Pierre, who has been living notoriously in St. Petersburg with Kuragin's dissolute son, Anatole, to settle on a career. Pierre's father, the incredibly wealthy Count Bezukhov, has in fact sent him to St. Petersburg to do just this. Pierre, however, does not wish to settle down just yet; he is having a glorious time (as we shall see). He wants to know why anyone should wish to fight Napoleon, his hero, "the greatest man in the world." He, for this reason, will not enter the army. He will only fight "on conviction." If no one fought except on his own conviction," says Andrew, "there would be no wars." Further, he says that he is going to war because the life he is leading "does not suit me." Lise enters. She speaks only in French (the Russian aristocracy of the time, regarding French civilization of the 18th Century as a model of social perfection, not only spoke and read and thought habitually in French, but many of them could speak only the merest fragments of Russian. This fact, for Tolstoy, a Russophile, was in itself symptomatic of the tendency of the aristocracy toward corrupt cultural values and evidence of its divorce from the "ferment of the people"). A brief altercation breaks out between Lise and her husband. She accuses him of having "changed." He orders her to be quite and suggests she go to her room. After this Pierre and Andrew go in, alone, to dinner. Andrew admits that he should not have married, that marriage has cut down his freedom to progress, to grow. He warns Pierre against marriage, berates society women as "selfish, vain, stupid, trivial in everything." But then, changing this tact ("his role is played out"), he urges Pierre to stop wasting his time in debauchery, and looks at his friend in a kindly manner - "yet his glance-expressed a sense of his own superiority." Pierre promises to reform, on his "honor."

Comment

This very important chapter serves to bring together at some length the two main characters of the novel. It is common critical knowledge that Pierre and Andrew are personae (or projections) of Tolstoy himself-two distinct sides of his character. In Prince Andrew we find the Tolstoy who had relished the atmosphere and glitter of society, who adopted its norms, sought to excel by its standards and suffered disillusionment with the whole charade. The small notations which accompany the character Andrew make us realize how ruthlessly accurate Tolstoy was with himself. He knows that others (remember the comment of the French emigre Vicomte to Hippolyte about Andrew giving himself the airs of a monarch) had probably seen through his posturing. In Andrew, too, we find that part of Tolstoy's character which expressed disillusionment and despair with what life had to offer, as well as his consciousness of his natural superiority-Tolstoy was, after all, one of humanity's greatest geniuses. In Pierre, conversely, we find that Tolstoy has placed those other characteristics he also had in great measure: a kind of radical simplicity of eye and heart, an almost peasant-like love of the basic facts of existence. Pierre's almost foolish naivete, his kindheartedness, his total lack of artificiality - these were not only characteristics of Tolstoy; they were characteristics he sought in others. Still, Pierre debauches, he drinks and acts irresponsibly, wastes his time, his opportunities, and his father's money. There is, really, no common vice that he does not freely indulge in, and then feel miserable about. Taken together then, Pierre and Andrew give us a good autobiographical portrait of the young man Tolstoy. Of course they do not exhaust Tolstoy-remember that each of the hundreds of characters are also parts of Tolstoy's gargantuan person.

CHAPTER THREE

Having given his word of honor to Andrew to reform and not to join the dissolute Anatole, Pierre immediately begins rationalizing his promise away. He cannot resist going. A wild party is going on at Anatole's apartment. There is even a bear present. The notorious rake and gambler, Dolokhov, has bet an English naval officer that he will drink an entire bottle of rum sitting on a third story window ledge without holding on. Before he is allowed to go watch, Pierre must drink all but a whole bottle of liquor himself. Later, Pierre rips the cross beam of the window frame out to give Dolokhov room. In a scene almost unbelievable in its tension, Dolokhov wins his bet. Pierre, swaying, hides his eyes, but peeps through his fingers. Then, overcome by the release of tension, and quite drunk, he offers to do the same thing, for nothing. The others restrain him. Anatole suggests a visit to some "actresses." Without a second thought, Pierre agrees, picks up the bear in his huge arms and the wild group goes off.

Comment

Having shown us society at its most artificial, then a domestic scene, Tolstoy, without apparently the least need to readjust his sights, takes us to a bacchanal. Although this kind of fertility of invention will go on and on, the reader might pause at the end of this chapter and reflect on the incredible number of actual characters he has met in such a brief time, and reflect on the fact that though he may have forgotten most of the names, he remembers the people, he remembers the settings. Isn't that like life itself? Although the art which has gone into his feat is, in the last analysis, the mystery of Tolstoy's genius, certain elements of it are available to the reader. First, there is control of the reader's eye and senses generally. Coming into Anatole's, "Pierre threw off his coat ..." There are "the remains of supper. A footman, thinking no one way him, saw drinking on the sly what was left in the glasses." Of the ear - "from the third room came sounds of laughter, - shouting, the growling of a bear, and general commotion." Then there is the absolutely natural and appropriate conversation; the picking of the precise detail which will link one moment with another so that the texture of the narrative preserves for the reader the illusion of the uninterrupted flow of time.

Again, there is the total conviction which each element offered by Tolstoy brings with it. How should a man who has just risked his life accept the money he has won by doing so? "The Englishman took out his purse and began counting out the money. Dolokhov stood frowning and did not speak." Now that is just right. Dolokhov does nothing merely for bravado; he has little money of his own, and lives by his wits. This is the way such a man would accept his wages. He has earned it. This brief detail tells us, as do thousands of others, that we can trust Tolstoy about life. He never sentimentalizes. He looks and sets down what he sees. Some have accused Tolstoy of being a primitive for this lack of distortion, in the same way, let's say as a camera is primitive. I think the reader will agree, however, that the ability to observe human actions with such unswerving fidelity is a mark of the highest artistry.

CHAPTER FOUR

In this chapter the setting shifts to Moscow, where we meet the large Rostov family, which includes Natasha, the major female character, her brother Nicholas, another central character, and Sonya, an impoverished niece of the Rostovs. It is Natasha's name day (that is, the feast day of St. Natalia). All day long guests arrive and depart. The Count issues invitations to all to attend dinner. We learn in the conversations among the principals the result of Pierre's visit to the "actresses": stopped by a policeman he had strapped the officer and the bear together and tossed both into a canal. For this he and Anatole and Dolokhov had been ordered out of St. Petersburg. We also learn that not only is Count Bezukhov dying, but that Pierre, as his favorite child, is probably heir to his incredible fortune.

Comment

Many of the Rostovs were patterned after Tolstoy's own family. Count Ilya Rostov is said to be modeled upon Count Ilya A. Tolstoy, the author's grandfather, a friendly, gracious man who depleted much of the family fortunes through hospitality of an **epic** variety. Natasha (whom we will meet in the next chapter), is said to be patterned on Tolstoy's youngest sister-in-law, Tatiana Behrs. Count Nicholas Rostov, the eldest son, is patterned after Tolstoy's father, Nicholas Tolstoy. Sonya is modeled on his aunt Tatiana who had looked his education; Countess Vera after Liza Behrs, another after sister-in-law.

CHAPTER FIVE

Still at the Rostov's, we finally meet Natasha, one of literature's greatest female creations. Like Cleopatra, who "hopped forty paces down the public street," Natasha "darted in and stopped short in the living room." She is thirteen, "black-eyed, wide-mouthed -, not pretty but full of life"; in fact, bursting with impetuosity. We also meet Boris, the same young man whose mother had accosted Prince Kuragin at Anna Sherer's soiree with a request that he get an appointment to the Guards. Here we also meet Nicholas and Sonya, who "wear their hearts on their sleeves" for each other. Nicholas is going off with the army. In the drawing room, Nicholas flirts with a young lady visitor; Sonya, on the verge of tears, gives him an angry look and goes out; Nicholas follows. In the conservatory among the plants, Natasha, hiding from Boris, sees them buss, then asks Boris to kiss her. When he does not, she kisses him. He declares his love, and says he wishes to ask for her hand in marriage, "in another four years." Natasha counts on her fingers. "Then it's settled?" "Settled," says Boris. "Forever?" "Till death itself?" Back in the reception room the Countess talks with her old friend, Boris' mother, who, tied up with lawsuits, is unable to provide the 500 rubles necessary to outfit Boris for his career. However, he is Count Bezukhov's godson. She will go to him and request assistance. Count Rostov asks that she invite Pierre, who is with his dying father, to his dinner.

Comment

The main thing to note in this chapter is the outline of Natasha's character: her intelligence, her impetuosity, her loving nature, her wildness, her lack of artifice.

CHAPTER SIX

Anna Mikhaylovna conducts her son Boris to Count Bezukhov's, urging him to be properly grateful and humble to his rich godfather. At the Count's, the hall pooter, "looking significantly at the lady's old cloak," treats them with scant respect. Finally, they are allowed to see Prince Kuragin, who, of course, is a relative of Bezukhov's, and is there attending to his own interests. Having done her a favor, he treats her with greater coldness than formerly. She must see the Count, however, and as one "used to suffering," insists on attending him. Kuragin, realizing he cannot get rid of her, gives in. She sits, "occupying the position she has conquered." Boris goes to see Pierre.

Comment

Anna is the mother who will do anything, literally anything for her child; wily, cunning, quickly adapting to whatever the situation demands, she gets her way. She will suffer embarrassment, degrade herself, call the hall porter "my friend," endure the rebuffs of Kuragin, the cold stares of the Count's niece, and get her way, and none of this is for herself. Her whole life is Boris. Notice the little touches in the masterly portraiture: "her trodden down shoes," the quickly assumed "expression of profound sorrow" which makes her son smile, her "concern" for the soul of the dying Count, a concern which will get her to the sickroom where her duty to Boris will be performed, and the rolling of the eyes. Here we have a woman whose only resource is her unconquerable will, a will directed by a single-minded devotion to her son's cause.

CHAPTER SEVEN

Boris visits Pierre in his apartment at the Count's, where for all practical purposes he has been exiled by his female cousins and Kuragin, and not allowed to see the Count. As Boris enters, Pierre is imagining he is Napoleon (at this stage of the book, his hero. Later he will come to detest him), and condemning Pitt, the English Prime Minister, to death. Boris, proud and sensitive, is most concerned to make sure Pierre does not think him a fly circling about the death bed of the wealthy Count. Pierre, the soul of impulsive goodness, admires the young man's character, accepts the invitation to dinner at the Rostov's, making "up his mind that they would be friends." Boris and his mother drive off. Boris wishes to know what the Count's attitude is towards Pierre - he is, as we see, like his mother, quite concerned about money and his future, even if Pierre is to be cut off in the will. "But why," he asks, "do you expect that he will leave us anything?"

"Ah, my dear! He is so rich, and we are so poor." "Well, that is hardly a sufficient reason, Mamma ..."

Comment

It is clear to the reader that Pierre's natural kindness does not permit him to see Boris' rather selfish, egotistic character; he, in fact, projects his own sensibility onto Boris. Also, that Boris, already committed by his mother's influence to see himself as special and superior, is blind to Pierre's unusual personality. He looks at him as one might view a big, overgrown child, thinking him rather stupid, not, so to speak, "in the know" about life. The opposites, artificiality and naturalism, are played upon again.

CHAPTER EIGHT

As is much of the novel, and perhaps, as Huxley says, all novels, this brief chapter is about money. Anna, returning from Bezukhov's, is given seven hundred rubles by Countess Rostova for Boris' outfit. Count Rostov is prodigal; his wife has only to ask for five hundred; he gives her seven. Note, however, that this economy is built on slavery. We hear that the great dinner is being prepared by one Taras, a serf for whom Rostov had paid a "thousand rubles."

Comment

Many critics have noted the sentence with which this chapter ends. Having given her old friend the money, the Countess and the Princess embrace and weep. "They wept because they were friends, and because they were kindhearted, and because they-friends from childhood had to think about such base things as money, and because their youth was over ... But those tears were pleasant to them both." Now, having read that, how can one ever regard elderly ladies weeping at weddings and family gatherings for no apparent reason, and not understand why they do it? Thus Tolstoy educates us about his subject - the human condition.

CHAPTER NINE

This chapter and the next give us the dinner at the Rostov's to celebrate Natasha's name day. We view another aspect of Russian society - this time a large, happy family gathering. Berg, Vera Rostova's intended, is present, so is Pierre, and Marya Dmitrievna, called "the terrible dragon" of Moscow society because, regardless of who is present, she speaks her mind on all subjects. As in Anna Sherer's salon, the focus darts from one conversation to another; we hear that the Emperor has issued a manifesto declaring war on Napoleon "to establish peace in Europe on a firm foundation"; we see that Nicholas is flirting with Julie Karagina (an heiress and friend to Mary Bolkonski, Prince Andrew's sister, whom we shall meet later); and that Sonya is consumed with jealousy. The atmosphere is gay, the drinks flow, there is much food and conversation. Everything, even the references to war and young men going off to the army, is spoken of with great joviality, the hilarity of the bright and happy moment uncontaminated by the horror and sadness which the future will bring.

Comment

Here for the first time Pierre, who after one bad marriage, will find the perfect marriage with Natasha, meets that gay and impulsive young thing, who unaccountably, "made him inclined to laugh." In Berg and the German tutor, as well as in the German Colonel of Hussars, with whom Nicholas is going off to war, we meet three examples of Tolstoy's pet aversion. Although, with notable exceptions (Napoleon for instance), Tolstoy treats the French soldiers with the same charity he bestows on the Russians, he seems not to have been able to abide the Germans. Berg is self-centered, pushy, and egotistical, a self-inflater, unaware that others have any interests at all. He is well suited to the cold, imperious Vera. The tutor is treated with great humor and sarcasm. Slighted by one of the footmen, who passes him by with the wine, this pedant is mortified; didn't they understand that he does not want to quench his thirst, that he is not greedy, but has, simply, "a conscientious desire for knowledge"? On the whole, however, what Tolstoy offers the reader here is a picture of ideal family life, for, according to Tolstoy, it is in the kind of commitment the Count and Countess make to another and to their children and relatives that happiness is to be found. One must save oneself from the corruption of egoism. This is another pair of opposites - the duty to others which brings freedom versus selfishness which destroys happiness.

CHAPTER TEN

The party at the Rostovs continues. Natasha finds Sonya sobbing because Vera has accused her of being ungrateful (she is, after all, a poor relation) and, out of spite, has told her (as it turns out, accurately) that Nicholas will not marry her but Julie Karagina.

Natasha soothes her, saying all will be fixed up to Sonya's satisfaction, remarking, as they go to sing for the assembled company, "that fat Pierre who sat opposite me is so funny!" Then, suddenly, "I feel so happy." Later, she talks to Pierre, aping the ways of a grown-up woman, conscious that Pierre is an adult who has been "abroad." Later the old Count Rostov dances wildly with Marya "the dragon," exerting himself wonderfully. It is a scene of intense, almost thunderous, joy.

Comment

Tolstoy, in creating the vast structure which is *War and Peace*, must constantly pick up the various pieces of the pattern, and establish patterns to come. We have seen how names mentioned and actions started in Anna Sherer's salon, at Anatole's party and elsewhere, are picked up again later. Note, for instance, how we found out about the results of Pierre's escapade with Anatole. Tolstoy must also prepare the reader for certain events in the future. Note here how he establishes the seeds of a relationship between Natasha and Pierre which will not blossom for a long time. This is a device known as foreshadowing.

CHAPTER ELEVEN

Count Bezukhov suffers, as the orchestra at the Rostov's is playing the sixth dance in a set, his sixth stroke. He cannot survive. The undertakers wait outside "in expectation of an important order." Prince Kuragin sees Catiche, Pierre's cousin, and explains that, since Count Bezukhov has written a letter to the Emperor legitimizing Pierre, Pierre will be heir to the Count's vast fortune. He and Catiche and her sisters will be cut off with little or nothing. He wheedles Catiche, who becomes almost deranged by the thought that she will not inherit what she has expected, into telling him where the Count keeps his papers. The implication is that Karagin will destroy the letter to the Emperor, and at this last moment deprive Pierre of his fortune and title.

Comment

The machinations of Kuragin in these moments, his craft and guile, serve to emphasize his self-serving character. At the same time, the **theme** of money and the importance of money is continued here, showing the corrupting effects it has on character. Even the "severe" and self-sacrificing Catiche turns into a tiger at the thought of being deprived of it. Two other elements of narrative technique may be noted here: the intense suspense created (Will Pierre be deprived of his fortune? Where is he? Why isn't he there protecting his interests?), and also Tolstoy's habit of contrast: a scene of gaiety alternated with a scene of tragedy.

CHAPTER TWELVE

Pierre and Anna Mikhaylovna (always attending to her interests) arrive at the Count's house. Going in the back way, Anna leads Pierre, who really has not grasped the significance of what is going on, directly to the antechamber outside the Count's room. She declares that she loves Pierre "like a son" and will "look after his interests." Everyone treats Pierre with deference. He feels that he is part of some "awful ritual" and that it is best to follow Anna's hints and directions. She leads him to the Count's bedside. The Count has just received the last sacraments of the Russian Church. He is surrounded by long-haired priests and relatives praying. Pierre, helping servants to move his father, suddenly realizes that his father is dying. Tears come to his eyes. He leaves.

Comment

Pierre's innocence of worldly ways is emphasized in this chapter. He cannot understand that people are scrambling for bits and pieces of the fortune, nor why they treat him with consideration. He seems to have many of the aspects of the "holy fool," a kind of saint who is so indifferent to worldly values as to seem a fool to those who hold such values. Another thing to note here is that Tolstoy, who rarely describes a setting at any great length, describes the Count's dying moments in great detail. This is done to bring the reader, with Pierre, to the verge of tears.

CHAPTER THIRTEEN

Count Kuragin, Anna, and Catiche struggle indecorously over the portfolio which contains the letter to the Emperor. Kuragin and Catiche must get to the dying Count and have him repudiate this will. Also, since there is another will leaving Catiche, her sisters, and Kuragin the fortune, we are given to understand that Kuragin will not hesitate, simply, to "forget" about the contents of the portfolio. It would be so easy. But Anna hangs on, literally. Machiavellian herself, she understands how deceitful others can be. But all this struggling is for naught. The Count's death is announced. Kuragin, who has gotten to the point of agitation in which he is "twitching," collapses; "Death is awful." "How often we sin," he says, "how much we deceive, and all for what? I am near sixty, dear friend … I too …" Anna makes sure that Pierre realizes his indebtedness to her, or tries to. He still does not understand what all the fuss been about.

Comment

Even though Kuragin is what might be called, in an ordinary novel, a villain, note here how Tolstoy preserves his humanity by giving him other dimensions. At death, he weeps, and sees himself for what he is; still, out of habit almost, he will continue politicking for position, currying favor, playing his elaborate game.

CHAPTER FOURTEEN

Now the scene shifts to the estate of the Bolkonskys, "Bald Hills," about a hundred miles outside of Moscow. This is the family estate to which Prince Andrew, in the first chapter, had made plans to bring his pregnant wife, Lise, while he serves in the army against Napoleon. Prince Nicholas (patterned on Tolstoy's maternal grandfather, Prince Nicholas Volkonsky), a general, extremely wealthy, is called "the King of Prussia." The Prince is a busy, well-occupied man, interested in all matters, practical and impractical; he is what is known as an "amateur savant," a man of the same model as, in our own country, for instance, was Thomas Jefferson. Without political influence, he is, all the same, highly respected and his opinions sought. He runs his estate on the principles of order, punctuality, and exactitude. Here we also meet Princess Mary, his daughter, patterned on Tolstoy's mother, who is much given to prayer, good works, and deep spirituality. This young lady is being taught geometry (as was Tolstoy's mother) by the Prince-but not too successfully. She loves him but fears him. In a letter from her friend Julie Karagina we hear that Nicholas Rostov has gone off to the army, about the death of Count Bezukhov, that Pierre is now "Count Bezukhov and possessor of the finest fortune in Russia," and that everyone now finds him most welcome and desirable. She, however, has no interest in "the poet," as she calls Pierre because of his dreamy ways. She also notes that there is a marriage plan for Mary (her correspondent), bringing back into the narrative the marriage arrangement suggested by Anna Sherer to Kuragin for his dissolute son Anatole. Marya, in turn, writes to Julie; she subjects herself to much critical analysis; she, concerned with her spiritual development and religion generally, looks on marriage "as a divine institution to which we must conform." She notes that she has seen a convoy of conscripts. "You should have seen the state of the mothers, wives, and children ... the sobs."

Comment

In this chapter Tolstoy is at great pains to establish the character of the Prince, the character of Mary, and the general atmosphere of Bald Hills. This is a well-run estate and well-run estates were of interest to Tolstoy, who, of course, had huge estates himself. Like the Prince, he too experimented with education and tried his hand at manual labor. In the Bolkonskys we are offered another, if quite different, example of the good people (those who are not egotists and are committed to work and service). Equally important is the use of the letters, which serve two purposes: to acquaint us rapidly with the character of Mary, and to act as a bridge or transition device in the narrative. We learn what is happening in Moscow, although we are now in a new setting.

CHAPTER FIFTEEN

Andrew arrives with Lise. Old Tikhon, the Prince's attendant, greets them. Not even the arrival of his son, however, is important enough to disturb the Prince's meticulously arranged existence. "He will get up in twenty minutes," says Andrew, alighting from his carriage and looking at his watch. Lise and Mary embrace and kiss-too enthusiastically. They hardly know each other. "Prince Andrew shrugged his shoulders and frowned, as lovers of music do when they hear a false note." Andrew visits his father while he is dressing for dinner. He outlines the plans of the coming campaign against Napoleon. Punctually at two o'clock (the clock is striking), the Prince goes into dinner. The talk - the Prince, is, after all, a retired general - turns to war again. He thinks nothing of Napoleon, that "Frenchy." He has only beaten "the Germans." He is not a "great general" - as Andrew has been maintaining - at all.

Comment

Although this first book has been concerned with family matters and social matters of one sort or another, the reader cannot but have noticed the casual but fairly constant references to war. Here, in this chapter, most of the conversation has to do with war. We are soon to leave scenes of domesticity; we are going with Andrew to war. In the next book the situation will be reversed; in war references to peace, just as in peace references to war, will keep us aware constantly of these major occupations of humanity. Note Lise's brief statement about the widow who has cried her eyes out. Not too far in the future, she will be, she thinks, a widow.

CHAPTER SIXTEEN

Andrew leaves to join Kutuzov, as his adjutant. Mary blesses him, gives him an icon (a religious picture) reminding him that God will protect him. She asks him to understand Lise, to be loving and kind. He says goodbye to his father; instead of giving way to the tears he wants to shed, the old man shouts "go, go." Lise, as Andrew expects, faints on his neck. He strides out the door.

Comment

In this, the final chapter of Book One, the fact established in the first chapter - that Andrew is going to sway-is realized. As do many other elements this organizes, gives unity to, the diverse pieces of material. Here, for the first time, the **theme** of religion and spirituality is introduced. We have seen before the ironic treatment of conventional piety as practiced by Boris' mother and Prince Kuragin. Here, in the contrast between the Voltairean (after Voltaire, the French rationalistic philosopher and religion baiter) atheism of the Prince, an atheism shared by his son, and Mary's profound and simple faith, we have Tolstoy's treatment of true religious faith. Andrew's character can be understood best, perhaps, as that of a man who has lost his faith and can find nothing to replace it. Hence, he does not understand life and can only be contemptuous and ironic.

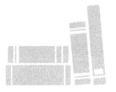

WAR AND PEACE

. . . .

CHAPTER ONE

Books Two and Three have for their background the campaign of 1805 which Alexander I of Russia, in alliance with Austria and others, carried out against Napoleon in an attempt to halt him. Already Emperor of France, King of Italy, and in control of the greater part of Europe, he was threatening England and was regarded as a threat to Russia. The particular event which caused Alexander to act was popularly held to be the execution of Conde, the Duke d'Enghien, by Napoleon. His story, you will remember, was told by the French marquis in Anna Sherer's salon. The setting for Book Two and parts of Book Three is Austria, along the Danube River. The campaign culminates in the battle of Austerlitz (December 2, 1805) in which the forces of Russia were beaten. The greater part of the action in Book Two is given to us from the viewpoint of Andrew, whose story we will now follow.

In this chapter a regiment of the Russian army, newly arrived in Austria, is reviewed by Kutuzov. In his retinue is Andrew who calls his attention to Dolokhov, who has been degraded to the rank of a foot soldier for his escapades, and is, in fact, wearing a non-regulation officer's overcoat. After the inspection, the troops march to bivouac areas singing.

Comment

Book One has dealt with society and family relations, introduced most of the characters, directly or indirectly, and given the reader a sense of the firm, continuing structures of human relationships. These might be called the normal activities of peace ceremony, the ritual activities of society, family life, love, death, money factors, drinking, dancing, ambition, and so on. Following the direction given us by the title itself, *War and Peace*, Tolstoy presents us with the activities of war: confusion, waste, hideous distortions of normal human relationships, the loss of the sense of meaning, etc. It will be recalled that Tolstoy often presents the reader with opposites: love-hate, joy - tragedy, happiness - unhappiness. It might be said that he is Hegelean in his approach to truth. Hegel, the eighteen-century German philosopher, proposed (to simplify his complex philosophy) that truth is dialectic, that is, it is neither one assertion nor its opposite, but both together; hence, to know anything we must take into consideration both movement and response, force and counterforce. It is his constant attention to this kind of pattern, in large and small events, that creates the terrible tension and sense of reality in Tolstoy.

CHAPTER TWO

At a meeting in Kutuzov's private rooms, various commanders are assembled to establish a plan of action. Kutuzov says, "If the matter depended on my personal wishes ..."

Comment

Right from the beginning (for these are the first words which Kutuzov speaks in the narrative) Tolstoy emphasizes his primary notion about the larger movements of history - "personal wishes" have very little effect on them. Kutuzov is Tolstoy's "hero" because he knows this. Napoleon, on the other hand, is Tolstoy's "villain" because he takes personal credit for the great actions in which he is merely involved.

To the place of the meeting comes "the unfortunate Mack," commander of the Austrian forces, chagrined that he is unrecognized. He is disheveled and near despair. Andrew leads him in to see Kutuzov. The general rumor is that the Austrians have been defeated. Andrew is quite changed in character from the man we knew at Bald Hills. He is fully engaged in his new career, serious, enthusiastic. Kutuzov has sent a letter praising him to Prince Bolkonsky.

CHAPTER THREE

The scene changes to a town in Austria called Braunau, where Nicholas Rostov is stationed with his regiment, the Pavlograd Hussars. Having returned from a foraging assignment, he greets Denisov, with whom he is quartered. This young man lisps. Telyanin, an officer who has sold Rostov a horse named "Rook," drops by to see them.

He is not well liked; he has shifty eyes. Shortly after he leaves, it is discovered that Denisov's money purse, which he had given to Rostov for safekeeping, is missing. Stung by the possible implication that he might be suspected, Rostov sets out after Telyanin, finds him at an inn where he is enjoying a meal, and accuses him. Telyanin trembling begs to be spared. Confused by the whole business, Rostov flings the purse at him and storms out.

CHAPTER FOUR

Rostov has accused Telyanin before the company commander of robbery and unexpectedly finds himself in hot water because of it. The commander, angered by the complications which proceedings will cause and realizing that the honor of the regiment will be impugned by association, accuses Rostov of lying. There is an impasse; neither side will give in. However, the news arrives that Mack's army has been routed; the regiment is ordered to move. The affair is forgotten in the excitement.

Comment

Rostov, who has been raised with the strictest notions of honesty about money, begins to discern that there are other more deeply rooted forms of righteousness. He, in fact, is being educated in the ways of the world. Don't forget that he has never been away from home before and still believes that all follow the same code of conduct which was the rule in his family. Now he is in a situation in which certain ideals, good in themselves, come into conflict. The question is: should Rostov swallow his pride in his integrity when such pride is in conflict with the general pride of the regiment? How Rostov answers this question, suggests Tolstoy, will have a great deal to do with what kind of man he becomes. You will remember, I'm sure, Boris and his mother in this connection and how they act to get what they want. Ultimately, Tolstoy says, it is all these small choices which go to form the character and identity of an individual.

CHAPTER FIVE

After Mack's defeat, Kutuzov's army retreats toward Vienna across the Enns River. Everything is in terrible disorder, civilians and soldiers crowd across the bridge escaping. Then there are only the Cossacks on the other side, scouting the empty country for the first signs of Napoleon's troops. Rostov dreams, pathetically, of being wounded, and, in these self-pitying circumstances, forcing an apology from his commander. The bridge is fired by his regiment; only a few persons are wounded.

Comment

Rostov, still the adolescent in the midst of the human cataclysm around him, can think only of himself. Note here how the focal point shifts, as it does so often in Tolstoy, from a distance which offers the reader all the panorama of action to individuals caught up in the swirl of the event itself. This double focus, near and far, is consistent with Tolstoy's assertion that we cannot see the whole truth except by such a device.

CHAPTER SIX

Kutuzov's army retreats along the Danube. At the town of Krems there is a small engagement in which the Russians are successful. Andrew hastens to Brunn to report, his enthusiasm enlarging the victory out of proportion. The reception of his news disappoints him. He is made to understand that it is hardly worth noting such a "victory."

Comment

Although this chapter is, as it were, an eddy out of the main stream of the action, it serves the purpose of showing how Andrew's awareness of the situation grows. He learns how unimportant individual lives are held in the overall scheme of things, that the bird's-eye view, say, of the historian, is essentially a different one from the view of the persons engaged in specific and particular acts. Such opposing views, following Tolstoy's plan, represent the polarities of human existence: the panoramic, grand scale view in which the individual is lost versus the personal view in which the grand plan is lost.

CHAPTER SEVEN

Andrew rests, after his hard ride, with Bilibin, an acquaintance in the diplomatic service. Bilibin questions, as might the French themselves, the value of the reported victory. As far as he is concerned, the campaign is over - the Russians might as well accept the fact and go home. Andrew, in spite of the defeat, is still enthusiastic about his hero Napoleon. "What an extraordinary genius." Bilibin thinks a secret peace is being negotiated with Napoleon.

Comment

Andrew, like Rostov, is being subjected to situations which will force him to mature. Not only does Tolstoy explore a situation by presenting opposite aspects of it; he also shows us various sides of events by the technique of parallelism. Although Andrew is the main character in this book, Rostov is seen to go through many similar experiences; each has his ideals questioned, each finds that his understanding of things is often wrong, each has a residue of idealism, or illusion, which reality has not been able to destroy. Compare Rostov's dream of glory with Andrew's "dream" hero. Both, says Tolstoy, are living in illusion. Such illusions must be eradicated.

CHAPTER EIGHT

It has been arranged for Andrew to present his report to the Emperor Francis of Austria. While waiting, he is entertained by some wealthy acquaintances, among them Hippolyte Kuragin who is attached to the diplomatic mission in Vienna. Andrew sees that Hippolyte is the "butt of this set." He wishes to get back to Kutuzov.

Comment

The foolish Hippolyte serves to remind us that the world of Pierre, Kuragin, the Rostovs, and Anna Sherer still exists.

CHAPTER NINE

Andrew is received by Emperor Francis and gets, contrary to his expectations, a warm reception. No sooner is this affair over when the news comes that "the scoundrel is again at our heels." Napoleon is, in fact, in Vienna, with not a blow struck. Andrew leaves for the army resolved, in his dreams, to save it.

CHAPTER TEN

Passing remnants of the fleeing Russian forces, Andrew, thinking of his high destiny, can only feel disgust. "It is mob of scoundrels -" At Kutuzov's headquarters he learns that an immense French force of almost a hundred and fifty thousand men is advancing. Advantage is taken of a three day truce to regroup and rest. Napoleon, suspecting a ruse, resolves to strike.

Comment

Napoleon's letter to Murat is authentic.

CHAPTER ELEVEN

Andrew, having begged Kutuzov to release him from his duties as aide-de-camp, attaches himself to Bragation, whose troops are facing Napoleon's army. He makes the rounds of the encampment and meets Captain Tushin, one of Tolstoy's "good people," who will be of some influence in Andrew's life. This captain commands a forward battery of cannon. The French lines are so close that the opposing troops can speak to each other.

Comment

At Sevastopol, where he himself commanded a gun emplacement, Tolstoy often noted, during truces established to gather in the dead, the seeming paradox that men, devoted to annihilating each other from a distance, acted toward each other on close contact as friendly human beings. This fact contributed heavily to his belief that if it were up to ordinary people, there would be no wars at all. The reader may recall the conversations between enemy troops in Crane's *The Red Badge of Courage.* During World War One, during brief truces, the German and Allied French soldiers were known to converse.

One of those speaking with the French troops is Dolokhov, the mad gambler. However, in spite of all this friendliness "the guns remained loaded ..."

CHAPTER TWELVE

Andrew, as the "eye" of the narrative, takes up a position from which he can view the coming engagement. The village of Schon Grabern is directly opposite. Thinking of things from an historical point of view, Andrew "imagined only important possibilities." As if to point up the emptiness of such abstract imaginings, a conversation between Tushin and another soldier takes place. They are, they say, afraid of what will happen to them. Just then there is "a whistle in the air." It is the start of the battle.

CHAPTER THIRTEEN

During the battle, Bagration inspects the area with Andrew. He says "very good" to everything, as if he knew exactly what was going on. Andrew notes that "Bagration tried to make it appear that everything that was done, if not by his direct command, at least in accord with his intentions."

Comment

Bagration is one of those people who consciously or unconsciously presume that their wills are directing affairs. Tolstoy's ironic point here, if course, is that such a view is nonsensical, egotistical, and even immoral. It indicates a notion of self-importance close to what the Greeks called hubris, or overweening arrogance, a kind of pride which seeks personal credit for the outcome of events which properly must be given to the gods. For this arrogance Napoleon is condemned; for its absence Kutuzov is praised.

CHAPTER FOURTEEN

Confusion is caused in battle by two commanders who do not understand each other's respective positions. Rostov's regiment is engaged. He is wounded. "Can something bad," he asks, "have happened to me?" He runs away.

Comment

Again the reader might be referred to *The Red Badge of Courage*, in which the young hero, Henry Fleming, runs off from his first engagement with the enemy.

CHAPTER FIFTEEN

The Russian troops are in a panic. No one, despite efforts, can halt the rout of the soldiers. However, Dolokhov has distinguished himself by taking French prisoners. So, too, has Tushin, by setting fire to Schon Grabern. Andrew arrives at Tushin's battery carrying orders for a retreat and helps to remove the two undamaged guns. In saying goodbye, Tushin finds his eyes unaccountably filled with tears.

Comment

As I have pointed out, Tushin is one of Tolstoy's "good people." He rides the tide, accepts life as it comes, is self-effacing, gentle, courteous, courageous. He does his duty. In Andrew who is a "seeker," he recognizes goodness of a kind different from his own. Tushin's goodness, in great measure, like Kutuzov's and Pierre's, is "natural"; Andrew must cut away layer after layer of self-deception and restraint before his goodness shows. In the midst of battle the point is made: in service to others lies salvation.

CHAPTER SIXTEEN

Retreating, "all gave … orders as to how to proceed. Tushin gave no orders …" The dead are abandoned, the wounded left behind. Rostov begs to be taken on Tushin's gun carriage. Later, confused, in pain, Rostov observes Tushin's kindness at the campfire; he performs all the necessary works of mercy: he gives water to the thirsty, food to the hungry, warmth to those without fire, sympathy to the discomforted, direction to the lost, and general goodwill without asking anything in return. Later, again underscoring his Christ-like character, Tushin does not defend himself when Bagration reprimands him about the loss of some of his guns. Andrew, disgusted that such a man, whose heroism he knows, is treated so shabbily, defends him to the commander.

His defense is received in silence. A scapegoat is needed. At the campfire Rostov dozes off and dreams of home, Natasha, his parents. When he wakes, he is alone. It is beginning to snow. "And why did I come here?" he asks himself. The next day, for some reason, the French do not renew the attack.

Comment

Here at the end of Book Two, Tolstoy uses the same kind of linking device as at the end of Book One. You will recall how, gradually, that part of the narrative focused more and more on war and Andrew's leave-taking. Here, Rostov's dream of home serve does direct the reader's attention to the next book, in which we will return as a matter of fact to Anna Sherer's salon again.

WAR AND PEACE

BOOK THREE

. . . .

CHAPTER ONE

On December 2, 1805, the battle of Austen City will take place. All events tend toward this. Now, however, the scene abruptly switches to Prince Vasili Kuragin and another soiree at Anna Sherer's (notice the patterning in Tolstoy's plan). Kuragin has taken very good care of his relative Pierre, using his influence to have him appointed a gentleman of the Bedchamber. He also brings it about that Pierre marries his daughter, the gorgeous, but amoral, Princess Helene. Pierre is embarked on a "career" in the diplomatic corps.

Comment

This chapter might well be called "How lamb, Pierre, is taken in hand by Fox, Kuragin, and delicately fleeced." Without for a moment losing his habitual world-weariness, Kuragin, a practiced confidence man, gives poor Pierre the impression that all his interest in him is benevolent, even if time-consuming. Pierre, confused by the fact that everyone treats him with such consideration, is only too happy to sign this and that. He has, of course, no head at all for business. Note, too, the contrast in Anna Sherer's behavior to Pierre. It is she who puts Helene in his way; Pierre regards the girl as stupid, but a magnificent woman. On Helen's name day the trick is accomplished. Six weeks later the two are married.

CHAPTER TWO

Kuragin, having settled Helene, now must settle the dissolute Anatole. For this purpose he advances on Prince Nicholas Bolkonsky with the idea of arranging a marriage between his son and Mary. Prince Nicholas has a very low opinion of Kuragin. The thought of his arrival generates still more "contemptuous ill will." He is so angry that when he learns the snow has been shoveled from the road in preparation for Kuragin's approach, he orders it scattered about again. In fact, he is rather eccentric, and so used to his own ways, that everyone is frightened of him, especially Lise (Andrew's wife). The ladies, when Anatole has arrived, cannot decide how to dress Mary. Alone Mary prays, "If it is God's will ..." let the marriage take place. She is plain, she is frightened; however, Christian resolution fills her, and she goes down to meet her suitor.

Comment

Two things might be noted here: the forced contrast between, on the one hand, Helene's worldly character mated with Pierre's innocence, and, on the other, Mary's spirituality placed against the corrupt Anatole. Having played upon one set of characters, now Tolstoy plays upon the other. Note also, the large part money plays in these arrangements, and the condition of women in such a society, who are used for such bargaining.

CHAPTER THREE

Now we find what is really bothering Prince Bolkonsky. Without really admitting it to himself, he does not wish to part from his daughter. He'll do nothing against the marriage, he decides, but "he must be worthy of her." Repeating this phrase, he enters the drawing room. He immediately embarrasses his daughter by telling her never to change her dress without his consent; "... she need not make a fool of herself, she's plain enough as it is." He questions Anatole briefly, dismisses him, brings Kuragin into a private room and screams at him "let her marry, it's all the same to me." Mademoiselle Bourienne, a French woman and companion to Mary, had often dreamed of being seduced by a Russian prince and marrying above her station. Well, here is the Russian prince (Anatole). She sets about pleasing him. Mary, also, is beginning-for he is there-to love him. How happy she is-a good friend in Mademoiselle Bourienne, a handsome future husband in Anatole.

CHAPTER FOUR

Bolkonsky, jealous, will not, he decides, allow his daughter to marry. He sees that Anatole is flirting with the Frenchwoman and decides to make use of this fact. The next morning, in a fury, he tells Mary that it is the Frenchwoman in whom Anatole is interested. Sure, he will marry Mary, but she will not be the real wife-her maid will be. Mary leaves him, horrified, goes into the conservatory and discovers Anatole and Frenchwoman embracing. Later, she goes to her father Kuragin, who, ignorant of what has taken place, and sure of himself, gaily urges her to decide Anatole's fate. Mary says, calmly, "My desire is never to leave you, Father, -----" "My vocation," she continues, "is to be happy with another kind of happiness, the happiness of love and self-sacrifice."

Comment

Here again, in Mary's utterance, Tolstoy's creed, happiness through self-sacrifice, is sounded. The reader must remember that Mary is based on Tolstoy's mother, and in her he placed the fountainhead of his salvation.

CHAPTER FIVE

The scene shifts to the Rostovs. A letter has just arrived from young Nicholas, who, you recall, was wounded. Sonya and Natasha talk about their mutual loves. Natasha confesses that she cannot really recall Boris. Sonya maintains the depth of her own love for Nicholas. Petya, the younger brother, remarks, offhandedly, that Natasha "was in love with the fat one in spectacles," referring, of course to Pierre. Now Natasha is apparently in love with her singing master. All the family writes letters to Nicholas "the hero," and the Count encloses six thousand rubles.

Comment

The subterranean relationship between Pierre and Natasha is hinted at; we see again Natasha's vibrant, loving character, and note, in passing, Boris' mother making sure her son is being taken care of.

CHAPTER SIX

The scene switches to Kutuzov's army. The Guards, with whom Boris and Berg (Vera Rostov's fiancee) are stationed, arrive from Russia. Nicholas Rostov visits Boris, who has his letter and money. The contrast between the clean and self-indulgent Guards and Nicholas's regiment, the Pavlograds, worn and muddy, is shown us. Boris has made may useful acquaintances, including Prince Andrew. The friends meet; it has been half a year since they parted. Nicholas asks Berg to leave the room so he can read his letters. Later Berg is asked back. Nicholas tells his story of campaign adventures. He means to tell the truth, but he begins to falsify. Andrew then enters. He has not met Rostov previously. Rostov implies that he is telling stories about being at the front and a duel is threatened. Nicholas is impressed by Andrew's coolness and wishes him for a friend.

Comment

Tolstoy maintained that true history could never be gathered from an individual's memories or memoirs, for the simple reason that men, consciously or unconsciously, falsify through the desire for self-glory, out of illusion, or merely because they do not know everything and fill in the gaps with inventions.

CHAPTER SEVEN

In this chapter the Emperor, Alexander I, who has traveled with Boris' regiment from Russia, reviews all the troops those freshly arrived as well as the battle tested, both Austrian and Russian. Again Tolstoy controls the huge scene, the arrays of men, the vast panorama, with deceptive ease. Every general and every soldier was conscious of his own significance, aware of being but a drop in that ocean of men, and yet ... "conscious of his strength as a part of that enormous whole." All day the troops assemble. Then the reader's eyes are directed to Olmutz, where "a group was seen approaching." A light wind sweeps over the entire army, the bannerets and standards are stirred.

Comment

Through many devices of description, direction and personification, Tolstoy enables us to see the huge army and gives us consciousness of its unity. The little wind, even serves its purpose. It makes the army one entity; it seems to shiver with joy at the approach of the Emperor. In its shout of welcome, it is amazed at its own power. Note how respectfully the Emperor is treated; "handsome," "kindly," "young" are the adjectives used. Now we focus through Nicholas Rostov's eyes and see the scene from the individual's point of view. Rostov, intoxicated with joy at the sight of the Tsar, thinks of him as majestic, almost godlike. Then "farther and farther" the Tsar moves off until only his plumes are visible. In the emperor's suite is Andrew, sitting his horse "indolently." Rostov thinks of his quarrel. "I love and forgive everybody now," he says in his enthusiasm.

Tolstoy here is able to give the reader, by focusing on Rostov, the ecstatic enthusiasm greater "than the winning of two battles would have made them." Rostov wishes to be ordered "into the fire this instant" to please the Tsar.

CHAPTER EIGHT

Boris goes to see the influential Andrew, hoping that this connection will lead to an appointment to Kutuzov's suite. Like mother, like son, the reader might comment. Andrew takes the young Boris in hand and introduces him to Prince Dolgorukov, an adjutant general. A council of war has just taken place in which, contrary to Kutuzov's advice, it has been decided to advance and attack Bonaparte. Dolgorukov has advocated the attack. Boris is "conscious that here he was in contact with the springs that set in motion the enormous movements of the mass ..." He desires to be near this power. Dolgorukov is, however, too busy to consider Boris' petition.

Comment

There is heavy **irony**, given Tolstoy's interpretation of history, in Boris' attitude toward "the springs that set in motion." Boris' own self-seeking nature is just the kind which, so Tolstoy suggests, mistakes the source of power. In fact, such men as Dolgorukov and Napoleon are mere puppets of "the ferment of the people."

CHAPTER NINE

Nicholas Rostov's squadron of mounted troops, commanded by Denisov, of the lisp, is ordered to the front. Halted, he watches the mounted Cossacks and infantry battalions go forward. He is afraid, as he had been before. However, his squadron is held in reserve. He hears the battle afar. Later, he hears that there has been a splendid victory. He is depressed. The Emperor approaches. Rostov is again filled with joy. The Tsar is going toward the battlefield. The victory has been vastly overrated: only a French squadron has been captured. This however does not stem Rostov's love for "the Tsar and the glory of Russian arms." It is just before the terrible battle of Austerlitz, one of the great battles of all history.

Comment

Tolstoy continues to focus on events through the naive and innocent eyes of Rostov. The counterpoint of Tolstoy's overall knowledge of the events of the day and the fragmented, individual knowledge of any given soldier contributes to the great **irony** of battle. Rostov is shocked, for instance, that a dirty and dying soldier is noticed by the Tsar who says, using a conventional phrase: "What a terrible thing war is." Yes, says Tolstoy, if anyone clears his eyes of "glory," he will see what a "terrible thing war is."

CHAPTER TEN

The preparations go on to meet the French forces. An envoy comes from the French proposing a meeting between Napoleon and Alexander. Dolgorukov is sent instead; when he returns he is closeted with the Tsar for some time. Then, for two days the troops advance until it is the morning of December second, the day of the battle of Austerlitz. Here, "just as in the mechanism of a clock," once started, the wheels mesh it with all the other wheels, so the great mechanical event set in motion on that day is really made up of thousands of minute human acts - "passions, desires, remorse, humiliations, sufferings, outbursts of pride, fear, and enthusiasms" - not the result of any individual's single will.

Comment

Tolstoy is writing not only a novel, but an **epic**. Here he uses an epic **simile** comparing the intermeshed actions of an historical event with the complicated interrelated wheels and gears of a clock. The reader will recall the use of the **epic simile** (for ironic purposes) in the first chapter of Book One, in which Anna is compared to a foreman in a factory, spinning the wheels of conversation.

Kutuzov is depressed: he does not feel right, his intuition is against the engagement. "The battle will be lost ..." he states flatly.

CHAPTER ELEVEN

Plans have been approved; the inexorable working out of these plans will be accomplished. A final council takes place, during which Kutuzov sleeps. The generals carp at each other. Prince Andrew, who has a plan of battle, is not able to present it. After the council, Andrew begins to speculate: perhaps Kutuzov is right, that thousands will die because of "court and personal considerations." Perhaps he, too, will die. This leads him to question the whole worth of his life: "Tomorrow everything may be over for me!" Still, there might be an opportunity for him to save the day: after all, Napoleon, still his hero, "the little corporal," once saved the day and that act started him on the road to becoming Emperor. He, Andrew, might even replace Kutuzov. Dear as his whole family is, he would give them all "for a moment of glory ..."

Comment

For the first time the reader is allowed to see into the heart of Andrew: he is ambitious, not as Boris, or Berg, or all the little men, but with a divine ambition to go down in history as a great man. For this reason he has lost interest in Lise and society; they do not offer him a battlefield grand enough in which to excel. The very question - "What is the use of all this if death destroys everything?" - he avoids. Sixteen years later it was to lead Tolstoy himself to the verge of suicide.

CHAPTER TWELVE

This same night as Andrew searches his soul, Rostov is on skirmishing duty in front of Bagration's detachment. The Russian campfires are aglow as far as the eye can see. The distance, where Napoleon waits, is foggy. Rostov, too, is full of dreams of glory, but on a much less grandiose scale; he only wishes the Tsar to notice him. As he rides through the brush his eyes close in sleep: he dreams of Natasha, of glory. He starts awake. In the distance there is shouting. It is Napoleon's troops, greeting their emperor. Rostov is ordered to check on this. He is shot at and returns. He asks to be assigned to the front lines on the morrow and his wish is granted. He hopes to be spent on a message to the Tsar. The chapter closes with a proclamation from Napoleon to his troop. It is a ringing declaration to stand fast.

Comment

Notice here, again, Tolstoy's favorite device is pairing, and by doing so, knitting together the parts of his fabric. Note, too, how long the suspense has been building up toward the great battle, and how our concentration is upon young Rostov and Prince Andrew. Will they survive it? we ask.

CHAPTER THIRTEEN

The day of the battle dawns. At five in the morning the troops are up and astir. It is cold and dark. The various squadrons, battalions, and regiments in unending streams move out to take up positions. Another **epic** simile comparing the soldier borne along by the current of humanity about him to the sailor borne along on the deck of his ship is here introduced. A great fog pours in. "Bushes looked like gigantic trees ... level ground like cliffs and slopes." The enemy might be anywhere. After an hour's marching, a sense of dislocation sets in; "where are we?" the men think. There is confusion. All the orders which, in the council chamber, looked so neat and clear do not work so well in the grim relatives of a battlefield-who could have predicted the fog? Then the action starts, not in the expected place at all. The fog begins to clear in the hills. Napoleon, standing on high ground with his marshals, can see everything. Just as he expected, half the Russian troops have descended into the flat country of streams and swamps. His intention is to attack on high ground. He is happy-aside from everything else, it is the anniversary of his coronation. At the right moment, with "his shapely white hand," he signals the action to begin. The focus shifts from Napoleon to Kutuzov (note again the contrast device of Tolstoy. Here we find the great opponents, **protagonist** and antagonist). Andrew is with him, excited, convinced that this will be his great day. He is ordered by Kutuzov to go stop the third division. Having done so, he returns to Kutuzov. All the Russians, with the exception of Kutuzov, are under the impression that Napoleon is six miles to the front, "according to the dispositions." The Tsar, with Emperor Francis of Austria, rides up and Kutuzov presents respects. The Tsar wishes to know why he has not begun. "I am waiting, Your Majesty," says Kutuzov. Then, unexpectedly, the French, thousands of them, are there. "Here it is! ... My turn has come," thinks Andrew. The terrible slaughter is on. The standard-bearer is wounded. Andrew runs to it; just the opportunity he dreamed of to gain glory is given him. He runs forward. Then in the confusion of hand to hand combat, he is hit. He falls. Above him is the sky, "nothing but the sky ... How was it I did not see that lofty sky before? ... Yes, all is vanity, all falsehood, except that infinite sky ... Thank God! ..."

Andrew is out of battle. Our attention shifts to Rostov who, directed to get to the Tsar, is riding along among the disordered troops. He is caught up in the frontal charge of the Horse Guards. He avoids this and wonders whether he should gallop after them. Later he is horrified to hear that "of all those brilliant, rich youths, officers and cadets, who had galloped past him on their thousand ruble horses, only eighteen were left after the charge." He meets Boris, then Berg (still, even in battle, talking only of himself). He rides off again, losing his sense of direction. Everyone is running. The Tsar himself has retreated. Why should he, Rostov, stay then? Everywhere the wounded lie "like heaps of manure." The French fire at him. He continues, still looking for Kutuzov or the Emperor. Then, finally and by accident he meets the Tsar, alone on a battlefield. He does not know what to do with this moment of glory, and rides away. Someone else offers to assist the Emperor to cross a stream. Rostov is filled, from a distance, with envy. By five that evening the battle has been lost. Andrew, lying bleeding where he has fallen, overhears Napoleon who is riding by. He still thinks of him as "his hero." Napoleon orders Andrew taken up to the dressing station. Later Andrew meets Napoleon, and the contrast between Napoleon's petty joy at his victory and the width and calm of the everlasting sky is brought home to Andrew. He has learned the great lesson.

Comment

Tolstoy shows in this chapter a magnificent control of his material. We might note the parallelism that runs throughout between Andrew and Rostov. Both dream of glory, Andrew to bear the standard in a decisive moment, Rostov to be noticed by the Tsar; each is granted his wish, but nothing turns out the way it was expected: Andrew lies wounded mortally and Rostov is filled with bitterness at not having the courage to aid the Tsar. There is a further parallel. Just as Rostov is brought face to face with his hero, so Andrew is brought face to face with his: in neither case is the result what they expect. Further, it might be stressed here how worthless, in Tolstoy's opinion, is all worldly ambition. The sky goes on, the overriding world of God and nature goes on in spite of all men's petty desires and ambitions. Even the "great" battle of Austerlitz is merely an ant's game.

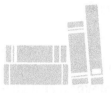

WAR AND PEACE

. . . .

BOOK FOUR

CHAPTER ONE

It is the year 1806. Nicholas Rostov returns home to Moscow on leave. It is a scene of joyous welcome. The world, notes Nicholas, in spite of his fears that it will have changed, is still the same. Sonya is there. Denisov is introduced. "Darling Denisov," shouts the irrepressible Natasha, hugging and kissing him. She is in love with someone else, as usual. Sonya has remained faithful to Nicholas; however, "he must be free." Vera points out that things have changed between Sonya and Nicholas, embarrassing everyone as is her unconscious habit.

CHAPTER TWO

Young Rostov, as a returned hero, quickly adjusts for the brief time of his leave to the attractions of Moscow life. He is no longer a child, but a hussar and a man about town; he goes to balls, to the races, to brothels. Old Count Rostov arranges a dinner for Bagration at the English Club (the gathering place of the wealthy nobility and gentry of Moscow. It was the seat of mild opposition to the Emperor's policies). He needs strawberries. Pierre can supply them. However, one notes that things are not too well with Pierre. Dolokhov, as a guest of the newly married Bezukhov, has compromised his beautiful wife Helene; Pierre is quite broken up. Well, says the Count, invite him to the Club. The news of Russia's defeat at Austerlitz is explained away by "the bigwigs" at the Club. Bagration, because one is needed, is honored as a hero. Kutuzov is abused. The word about town is that Andrew is dead.

Comment

Here, oblique reference is first given to Pierre's difficulties with the amoral Helene. His marriage will end in divorce. Note, too, Count Rostov at his favorite occupation-spending all his money on hospitality.

CHAPTER THREE

The dinner for Bagration takes place at the English Club. Pierre, his hair long, without spectacles, looks "sad and dull." He is growing contemptuous of self-serving condescension. Bagration is presented with some atrocious verses in Russian to honor him. The Emperor's health is drunk, as is the health of dozens of others. At a proposal of a toast to himself, Count Rostov, simple-hearted man that he is, weeps outright.

CHAPTER FOUR

Now the narrative concentrates on Pierre, who sits opposite Dolokhov; he is eating and drinking much. He has changed indeed; gloomy, withdrawn, depressed. He had received an anonymous letter that morning-we suspect from Boris' mother-suggesting Helene's infidelity with Dolokhov. Now he cannot look at Dolokhov. At this point Dolokhov, insolent as ever, proposes a toast "to the health of handsome women" - he looks at Pierre - "and their lovers." A moment passes. Pierre has been presented with a paper. Dolokhov takes it from him. Pierre, aroused by this nastiness, says "You --- ! you --- scoundrel! I challenge you!" At this moment he realizes his wife's guilt. "He hated her and was forever sundered from her." Arrangements are made for the duel. The next morning they meet. Pierre has never held a pistol before, and he does not have his glasses. He wants to get it over with; he does not care one way or the other.

Comment

In another masterpiece, *Anna Karenina*, Tolstoy was to explore in great depth the whole complicated notion of marital infidelity. Here, both Helene and Dolokhov are without moral values. They are hardly human in the Tolstoyan meaning of the term. Note, too, how subtle Tolstoy is: the reader will recall in the **episode** of the window sill that Pierre had challenged Dolokhov's feat.

CHAPTER FIVE

The duel begins. The affair, as Pierre feels, seems to be "taking its course independently of men's will." A complete child in these matters, he shoots. By pure luck he hits Dolokhov who falls into the snow; he runs forward to help him but Dolokhov still has his shot. Pierre must stand not ten paces away awaiting Dolokhov's careful aim. Pierre, "with a gentle smile of pity and remorse," waits, his broad chest exposed; he will not turn away. The shot comes-a miss! "Folly ... folly! Death ... lies ..." says Pierre stumbling off in the snow. Dolokhov weeps for his mother, "my adored angel mother." This bully and brawler, it turns out, lives in Moscow with "an old mother and a hunchback sister, and was the most affectionate of sons and brothers."

Comment

The complexity of human behavior is brought home to us with great force in this chapter, where the reader's sympathy is quickly pulled from Pierre to the improbable Dolokhov.

CHAPTER SIX

In thinking over his marriage, Pierre realizes how vulgar and cheap Helene is. He blames himself for succumbing to her beauty; he had never loved her. He had lied. Now he is being punished. Confronted, Helene is unrepentant. Pierre, in a fury, brings down a marble slab and smashes it to pieces. Had she not run out of the house he might have killed her. A week later, he settles the greater position of his estates upon her (it is after all what she wished), and leaves for Petersburg alone.

CHAPTER SEVEN

In Bald Hills, two months after Austerlitz, after all channels of information have been exhausted, Prince Bolkonsky, Mary, and Lise conclude that Prince Andrew has been killed. The old general is beside himself with pain and fury. He is dying of grief. Nothing interests the tireless old man now.

CHAPTER EIGHT

Lise, Andrew's little princess, is on the point of delivering his child. The labor pains - "the most solemn mystery in the world" - begin. No one sleeps that night. The snows of March scatter over the house; the wind beats the casements. In the dark someone drives up the avenue. Mary, thinking it is the doctor, hastens out. She hears a vaguely familiar voice. It is Andrew, returned.

Comment

The reader has been in ignorance of Andrew's fate since last seeing him before Napoleon at Austerlitz. In Moscow we have heard that he is dead. So, we are just as surprised of his return as his sister. Tolstoy is able to keep the reader, who knows more than Mary, in this state suspense because of the confusion of rumors in Moscow where we heard so much falsehood-if all the glorious feats are lies, so may be the report of Andrew's death.

CHAPTER NINE

Andrew kisses Lise. "My darling," he calls her - for the first time. He is sent from the room. A baby cries. There are screams. It is Lise "the little Princess"; she is dead. But Andrew has a son.

Comment

The reader, so little does he expect it, is as numbed by Lise's death as is Andrew. At this point the chronicle dimensions of *War and Peace* begin to become apparent. We have now three generations of the Bolkonskys before us.

CHAPTER TEN

Young Rostov, back in Moscow, becomes quite friendly with the recovered Dolokhov, whose mother thinks him "too noble and pure-souled for our present, depraved world." In fact, his character is more complex than we might have thought. He has a curious sense of justice: all women he says "are venal." If he could meet a good woman (such as his mother) he would give his life for her. Rostov brings him to his household where all like him except Natasha, for whom he is "unnatural." Pierre was right, in the duel. Besides, Dolokhov has taken a fancy to Sonya. In fact he seems to love her. The time is drawing near, however, for the young men to return to the army.

Comment

Napoleon has been so successful that for the first time the Russians must worry about their own frontier.

CHAPTER ELEVEN

On the third day after Christmas the young people assemble at the Rostovs. "Never had so much love been in the air ---" Dolokhov proposes to Sonya who declines his offer. Nicholas' feeling for Sonya is renewed by the idea that she has refused the "splendid, noble fellow" for him.

CHAPTER TWELVE

A ball takes place in Moscow. The Rostovs attend. Natasha, in her first long dress, falls in love with "everyone" at first sight.

She dances with Denisov (of the lisp). She falls again in love - this time with Denisov, who dances magnificently.

Comment

If the reader will recall how musical a house the Rostov's is, and that the old Count Rostov is an exuberant dancer, he will not think it strange that Natasha should be struck by Denisov, in spite of his lisp.

CHAPTER THIRTEEN

Nicholas is invited by Dolokhov, who will not come to the house "for reasons you know of," to a farewell supper. Nicholas finds Dolokhov gambling. Against his better instincts, he sits at a table with the notorious gambler. In a brief time Nicholas has lost 43,000 rubles. He is ruined and at Dolokhov's mercy. He promises the money for "tomorrow."

Comment

Tolstoy was himself, as a young officer, a notoriously unlucky gambler, who lost huge sums of money at a sitting. Here he recreates all the fascination and tension of such a game. Dostoevsky, the great Russian novelist, was also consumed by the passion for gambling. Certainly not even he, in the novel *The Gambler*, has been able to present more realistically this compulsive psychology of men like Dolokhov, nor the quicksand struggles of those who, like Nicholas, try to recover their losses.

CHAPTER FOURTEEN

Nicholas returns home. Natasha sings. Listening to her, Nicholas realizes that "this is life," that Dolokhov's values are false, that all money, honor, anger are false.

Comment

Nicholas is deceiving himself. He wishes life to be different than it is because he has gotten himself into a mess. Still, in art, represented here by Natasha's singing, Tolstoy suggests, before he repudiated this belief, man may discover a symbol of peace and truth and happiness.

CHAPTER FIFTEEN

Nicholas asks the large sum of money from his father, who, although shocked, promises to raise it. Denisov proposes to Natasha, who is directed by her mother to turn him down with thanks-she is too young. Denisov leaves for his regiment. Nicholas, having finally sent Dolokhov the money, leaves, too, for Poland where his regiment is quartered.

Comment

Again the reader's attention is directed to way by the young men's leaving.

WAR AND PEACE

. . . .

BOOK FIVE

CHAPTER ONE

The story of Pierre is here continued. Since the duel with Dolokhov, he has been in intense spiritual agony, questioning the value of human existence. At a wayside station waiting for a change of horses, he ponders more deeply. A fit of despair seizes him: "All we can know is that we know nothing. And that's the height of human wisdom." Another traveler comes to the inn, "a short, large-boned, yellow-faced, wrinkled old man ..." On his shriveled hand he wears a strange ring with a seal representing a death's-head. Pierre is fascinated by him and feels the need to speak to him. Unexpectedly, the stranger addresses him by name, fixing strange eyes upon him. He knows of Pierre's "misfortune" and offers to help him. He is a Mason. He challenges Pierre's view of life as made up of delusions: he does not believe in God, therefore he is unhappy. He offers to lead him to happiness. God is "not to be apprehended by reason, but by life." Pierre must purify his life before he can attain "wisdom," which is "the science of the whole." The traveler leaves, first giving Pierre directions to meet one of the Brothers of Freemasonry in St. Petersburg.

The old man, Pierre finds, is named Bazdeev, one of the leading figures among the Masons.

Comment

Just as Prince Andrew, under more dramatic circumstances, had found his whole life meaningless, now Pierre, from a different set of causes, comes to the same conclusion. The mysterious Bazdeev points him in the right direction. He must give up his present life-materialistic, purposeless, and vain - and pursue wisdom. The questions which confront Pierre in this chapter were the questions which confronted Tolstoy all his life.

CHAPTER TWO

In Petersburg, Pierre reads Thomas a Kempis, a Christian mystic of the fifteenth century whose book, *The Following of Christ*, is one of the most famous of all works of devotional literature). He is filled with joy. He is invited to become a member of the Brotherhood, and, in a long, detailed ceremony, is initiated. After the ceremony, "Pierre felt as if he had returned from a long journey ..., had become completely changed, and had quite left behind his former habits and way of life."

CHAPTER THREE

Resolved to retire to his estate and devote himself to the welfare of his serfs, Pierre shows the door to Prince Kuragin, his father-in-law, who has attempted to reconcile him to Helene. But Pierre recognizes that Helene will tempt him back to the life he despises. He departs for the country.

CHAPTER FOUR

At Anna Sherer's the talk is all about Pierre's duel and his rupture with his wife; he is blamed for both disasters. Helene is the pet of society because of her misfortune. Here at Anna's soiree "the cream of really good society" is talking about the defeat of the Prussian forces at Jena, and the entrance of Russia into the second war with Napoleon. Boris, who has been steadily climbing the ladder of ambition, is, in fact, the guest of honor. He has just arrived as a special messenger from the Prussian army. He is an aide-de-camp to "some important personage" and seeks "the acquaintance of only those above him in position and - therefore - of use to him." He has not once visited the Rostovs. At Anna's he is seated near Helene, who invites him to come see her. he accepts.

Comment

Tolstoy's special abomination was "society." Here, as usual, he pictures the habitues of Anna's salon as selfish, egotistical, self-seeking, and foolish. In a sense, although two years have passed since we first met Anna Sherer, she is precisely the same. All the "good" people in Tolstoy change - they are open to change, because they are alive. The "bad" people, being ignorant and blind, cannot change.

CHAPTER FIVE

Boris visits Helene at her home. He is at first ignored. Later, when he is leaving, she invites him to dinner. "During that stay in Petersburg, Boris became an intimate in the Countess' house." No wonder, Boris and Helene are ideal companions for each other.

CHAPTER SIX

The narrative returns to life at Bald Hills. Old Prince Bolkonsky has been put in charge of conscription. The war with Napoleon rages near Russia's frontier. Prince Andrew has named his son Nicholas after his father. Princess Mary spends most of her time with the child, who is now in high fever.

CHAPTER SEVEN

A letter from Bilibin, Andrew's friend in the diplomatic service, summarizes the events of the Prussian campaign of Napoleon. Andrew, concerned about the sick child, crumples the letter and tosses it away. He is called to the nursery, convinced that the child is dead. However, the fever has broken. "Yes," says Andrew with a sigh, "this is the one thing left me now."

CHAPTER EIGHT

The narrative returns to Pierre who is on his estate at Kiev in southern Russia. He assembles his stewards and explains the great plan he has developed to free his serfs immediately. His plan is met with distrust. Pierre has no head for business. Even though his income is enormous, it is not sufficient to allow him to live within his budget. Also, he becomes distracted by the social life of the district. His ambition to reform withers away. He resolves to return to Petersburg, visiting his estates on the way to see how his plans have been carried out. On all the estates' affairs appear to be going well: buildings for schools and hospitals are erected or going up, and deputations of happy peasants meet him and thank him. "How easy," he thinks, "to do good." However, what he does not know is that his chief steward thinks the whole business is "insane," and is doing everything in his power to prevent the freeing of the serfs.

Comment

When Tolstoy took over his estates he, too, attempted to free his serfs and was met with the same species of suspicion, indifference, and actual hostility. Much of the experience which Pierre undergoes is directly transcribed from the events of Tolstoy's own life.

CHAPTER NINE

Pierre is in a happy, if deluded, state of mind. He goes to visit Prince Andrew, whom he has not seen for two years, at his small estate of Bogucharova. Everything is tidy and efficiently run. Andrew, in contrast to Pierre's lack of business sense, has a head for management. Pierre is impressed by the bareness of the surroundings in which Andrew lives. Much has happened in the years of separation. They are constrained with each other. They talk of their new attitudes toward life. Andrew regards Pierre's benevolent outlook with an ironic smile. Their attitudes toward goodness are quite opposed: Pierre holding that it is attained by active nourishment of all the people in mind, spirit, and body; Andrew maintaining that what one wants is merely to avoid evil since one cannot know what the "good" is.

CHAPTER TEN

The conversation between the friends continues in the carriage driving them to Bald Hills. Pierre insists that happiness can only be attained through "equality, brotherhood, and love." At a river, they must take a ferry raft. When the raft arrives on the other bank, the two are so engrossed in talk of heaven, eternity, the afterlife, death and goodness that they do not disembark. The sun is sinking, its reflection slides on the broad, still, silent waters. "It is true, believe it!" Pierre whispers. "Yes, if it only were so," says Andrew. Then he looks at the sunset sky, the same "high, everlasting sky he had seen while lying on the battlefield." The old feelings stir once more. "His meeting with Pierre formed an epoch in Prince Andrew's life. Though outwardly he continued to live in the same old way, inwardly he began a new life."

CHAPTER ELEVEN

Coming to Bald Hills, the friends cause a stir among a group at the entrance. Andrew identifies them as pilgrims, "God's folk," to whom Mary, in this one thing disobeying her father, gives alms. Now, however, the old Prince is away conscripting for the army and the "holy folk" have invaded the house. Neither Pierre nor Andrew can take the pilgrims' talk of wonderworking miracles seriously, as can the simple-hearted Mary.

Comment

At Yasnaya Polyana, Tolstoy's estate, such pilgrims were often harbored during the author's childhood. In the preceding chapters he has given a profound analysis of the true nature of Christ's mission, of the meaning of religion. Here, in contrast, he gives us a picture of those who, although they have right intentions, are led astray by the accidentals of ritual, sensation, and wonders. Tolstoy never denied that he thought much of the outward practice of religion was close to mere foolery. Still, among such people as these, Tolstoy finds greater merit than he allows to the inhabitants of Anna Sherer's salon.

CHAPTER TWELVE

Prince Bolkonsky arrives and greets Pierre affectionately. He is in good spirits. They talk of war, Pierre maintaining there will come a time when there will be no more wars. "Old women's nonsense," says the old general. Father and son talk business: "the marshal, a Count Rostov, hasn't sent half his contingent. He came to town and wanted to invite me to dinner-I gave him a pretty dinner!" Pierre's visit comes to an end. All speak well of him.

Comment

Here, in an aside, another link is established: Count Rostov is referred to. In the next chapter we will pick up Nicholas Rostov's narrative. Note the telling detail about Count Rostov's dinner invitation. Here too, at Bald Hills, Pierre, who, one must remember, has had a lonely life, gets a glimpse of the joys of family. In such family happiness he will eventually find peace of mind.

CHAPTER THIRTEEN

Returned from his leave, Nicholas feels the bond of comradeship that binds him to his regiment. "Here, in the regiment, all was clear and simple." He knows his place. Decisions are made for him. The campaign against Napoleon continues. The Pavlograd regiment is stationed near a ruined German village. It is April.

There are few provisions. The crops have been ruined. Men starve. In spite of this life goes on. Rostov takes care of a starving Polish family. His friendship with Denisov is strengthened because of Denisov's love for Natasha.

CHAPTER FOURTEEN

Denisov and Rostov are living in an earth hut. The soldiers are starving, in fact living on noxious roots. Unable to stand the thought of his men not being fed, Denisov resolves to do something about it. He leads a detachment and seizes a provision transport from his own army. Biscuits are dealt out to the men. The next day the regimental commander sends for Denisov. He is to be put on trial for robbery. Who is the Commissioner in charge of provisions? Telyanin, who had stolen Denisov's purse once. Denisov hits him. This is a serious affair: Denisov is to be court-martialed and the regiment handed over to the next in command. But Denisov is wounded first and is put in the hospital.

Comment

Notice how Telyanin crops up again in the narrative, robbery being connected with him almost as an identification.

CHAPTER FIFTEEN

The great battle of Friedland is fought in June, after which an armistice is signed. Rostov, on a leave of absence from his regiment, visits Denisov in the hospital. It is a horrifying experience: conditions are terrible, the stink of putrefying flesh hangs in the air, there is typhus, the sick and wounded lie on straw and over coats on the floors, men scream for death, the dead are not removed. Here he finds Tushin, the battery officer; he has lost an arm. Denisov has changed. His wound is not yet healed. He can think only of his coming trial for robbery. He will not "grovel" to get himself off. Finally, however, he decides to petition the Emperor for pardon and asks Rostov to handle his request.

Comment

Tolstoy had been horrified by the treatment of the wounded in the Crimea when he served there. The reader will recall that it was to the Crimea that Florence Nightingale went with the first contingent of women to nurse the wounded and sick.

CHAPTER SIXTEEN

Rostov rides to Tilsit with the letter to the Emperor. Here Napoleon and Alexander are to meet to discuss peace terms. Boris has inveigled an appointment to be present: "I should like to see the great man," he says. He sees the great personages arrive and is filled with enthusiasm. He notes how everyone acts, seeks out the names of all in attendance. When the Emperors go into the conference he looks at his watch and does so again when they come out. He notes all this down, along with everything else he regards as having "historic importance." The aides-de-camp of the various armies fraternize. Rostov visits him and is unpleasantly struck by the presence of French officers, whom he still regards as enemies. Boris, Rostov notices, is annoyed at his arrival but covers this up with a smile. He asks Boris' help in presenting Denisov's petition to the Emperor, but sees that Boris is reluctant. His childhood friend has indeed changed a great deal, and not for the better.

CHAPTER SEVENTEEN

On the next day, June 27, the preliminaries of peace are signed. It is not a good time to present a petition. Rostov leaves Boris and wanders about the town. He is in civilian clothes, without permission to be here at all. He decides to seek the Emperor out personally. He meets a general who is known to him. The general takes Rostov's letter to the Emperor who, however, will do nothing. The law is stronger than he is.

CHAPTER EIGHTEEN

The two emperors meet in the town square. They dismount and shake hands. A Russian soldier is decorated with the Legion of Honor by Napoleon. Later there is drinking and carousing among the soldiers. The war is over; they can be friends. Rostov, however, is not joyful. He watches the banqueting from the sidelines. He is filled with "terrible doubts," contrasting in his imagination the filth and dirt of the hospital with the magnificent scene before him. Here were the emperors chatting away in the friendliest fashion. "Then why those severed arms and legs and those dead men?" These thoughts frighten him. He goes to a hotel and joins some officers he knows in a drinking party. Drunk, confused by everything, he shouts, "If once we begin judging and arguing about everything, nothing sacred will be left. - Our duty is to do our duty, to fight and not to think!" He orders another bottle. The Fifth Book ends.

Comment

Peace, temporary and brief, comes. For the next few years we will follow the fortunes of our various heroes and heroines without the terror and passion of war in the background. Here, in this final chapter of Book Five, Rostov's adolescence comes to an end with the insight, which he tries to suppress, that his great and good hero, the Emperor Alexander, is really no better than the "demon" Napoleon, that they are both equally indifferent to justice and goodness as these pertain to ordinary men. A major portion of his education, and ours, is over.

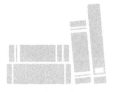

WAR AND PEACE

BOOK SIX

. . . .

CHAPTER ONE

Napoleon and Alexander are now allies. There is talk of
Napoleon marrying one of Alexander's sisters. But, for the
most part, "real life, with its essential interests of health and
sickness, toil and rest, and its intellectual interests in thought,
science, poetry, music, love, friendship, hatred, and passions-
went on as usual ..." Andrew has remained in the country for
the past two years. He has carried out many reforms on his
estates, not with the impulsive enthusiasms of Pierre but with
the methodical commitment to duty which is an expression
of his new-found philosophy of life. He is still deeply scarred
from his disillusionment with war, his wound, and the death of
his wife. A gentle melancholy pervades his outlook on life. On
a visit to one of his estates in earliest spring he passes a still
leafless, ancient oak. The oak seems to support, in its condition,
his view of things: don't be led astray by the illusion of spring,
it says; all hope is illusion. Yes, thinks Andrew, not unhappily,
he must simply live out his life, "content to do no harm." Weeks
later, Andrew goes to visit Old Count Rostov at that gentleman's

country estate. The day is beautiful. He sees a young girl running and laughing (it is Natasha) and feels "a pang." Count Rostov insists Andrew stay the night. He cannot sleep, opens the great windows, and leans there looking at the moon drenched garden. He hears girlish voices from the rooms above and recognizes one. Disturbed by new emotions, he finally goes to sleep. Next day on the way home, he passes the oak, It is in full, dense leafage, "transfigured." Andrew is filled with a sense of "joy and renewal." Life is not over. He is just thirty-one. He decides to go to Petersburg.

Comment

This chapter, full of beautiful and accurate descriptions of the earth in spring, is an appropriate setting not only for Andrew's reawakening to life, but of the upward impulse of the whole book.

CHAPTER TWO

Andrew goes to Petersburg, bringing with him a plan for the reform of army regulations over which he had been working during his country retirement. It is August of 1809. Soon he is caught up in the round of life in the Emperor's city: he visits court; is interviewed by Count Arakcheev, in charge of reorganization of the army, who rejects his plan; meets Speranski, the Emperor's advisor, a man devoted to "reason" above all things, who gets Andrew an appointment to the Committee on Army Regulations as Chairman of the section on Personal Rights.

Comment

Tolstoy, during his service at Sevastopol, drew up such a plan for reform in the army, but never submitted it. However, nothing he ever did or experienced went to waste.

CHAPTER THREE

The narrative now doubles back in time to early 1808, where Pierre's story had left off. On his return to Petersburg, Pierre had become more deeply involved in the work of the Freemasons. His life now continued as before, however, "with the same infatuations and dissipations." The great moment of illumination has passed. The members do not seem to him to be carrying out the great humanitarian projects for which the movement was designed. He delivers a speech to them calling for reform and a rededication to ideals. It is not well received. Depression sets in. At this point he receives a letter from Helene, his estranged wife: she will be in Petersburg for a few days. Will he receive her? In his diary, he records that he is now living again with his wife. He experiences a feeling of regeneration.

Comment

Note the continued use of parallelism; Andrew and Pierre are restored to a positive view of life, regenerated.

CHAPTER FOUR

Without further ado, the brilliant but rather stupid Helene establishes a salon which becomes the center of fashionable society. From time to time Pierre attends "as he would a theatre," bemused, indifferent, distanced. He bothers no one; society regards him as a curious but harmless "crank." Boris, who has attained "great success in the service," is conspicuously present. This fact makes Pierre uneasy; he does not wish a repetition of the Dolokhov **episode**. At the same time deep spiritual struggles are taking place in his soul.

Comment

Tolstoy sums up Helene's whole character in a phrase imputed to Napoleon: "C'est up superbe animal" (that's a superb animal). His own disgust with high society is revealed as the salon of Helene is analyzed for us with sharp irony and sarcasm.

CHAPTER FIVE

This chapter records Pierre's spiritual thoughts in excerpts from his diary. He asks God again and again to aid him in suppressing his sensual nature.

Comment

These extracts from the fictional diary of Pierre had their model in the entries Tolstoy made in his own diary. It is noteworthy that much of Pierre's diary is concerned with transcribing his dreams, as if to imply that the greater portion of Pierre's struggles occur below the level of consciousness. This device of using dreams in fiction to embody the subconscious drives of characters gives the author an opportunity he would not otherwise have of presenting certain material. Note, too, the contrast between the surface existence of Helene and the deep existence of society's "crank."

CHAPTER SIX

The Rostovs' story is continued. Because of the inordinate hospitalities of the old Count, the monetary affairs of the family are shaky. The Count has come to Petersburg seeking an official post which will increase his income. Soon after their arrival, Berg (the officer whom we met early on in the book, the one who imagines that no one has any concerns but those which involve himself) proposes to Vera, the eldest daughter of the Rostovs, and is accepted. Berg has gotten on. He is a captain, and holds some lucrative posts in Petersburg. He wishes, however, to do well for himself and maintain a proper home. He goes to the embarrassed and deeply mortgaged Count for information on Vera's dowry. Wishing to end the interview, the Count promises him exorbitant sums of money, which he cannot really afford.

Comment

When a girl was married, her parents provided her with a dowry, or, if you will, what amounted to a separate income for life. In effect, this income did not belong to the husband, though, in practice, most husbands regarded it as theirs.

CHAPTER SEVEN

Natasha is sixteen, "the very year to which she had counted on her fingers with Boris after they had kissed four years ago. Since then she had not seen him." Now, in Petersburg, he visits them. Despite himself, despite the fact that marrying her, an impoverished girl, would ruin his "career", Boris is attracted. He continues to visit, stops seeing Helene, who writes him reproachful notes.

CHAPTER EIGHT

Natasha comes to her mother's room to talk about Boris. The old Countess cautions her, pointing out that there can be no wedding, because, among other reasons, Natasha does not love Boris, and his frequent visits are only hurting her chance with other young men. Well, let Boris come if he enjoys it, says Natasha. She is really just full of life, in love with love. Boris is not to her taste; "he is narrow, like the dining room clock ..." Now Pierre, "he is square, fine." In her own room in bed, she thinks how charming, intelligent and vivacious she is. She is entirely spontaneous in her joyful self-appreciation. Next day the Counters talk with Boris; he stops coming.

CHAPTER NINE

Natasha attends a grand ball at which the Emperor is present. So is Helene, and her dissolute brother, Anatole, Princess Mary's erstwhile suitor. Pierre, "the stout one in spectacles" is present, as is Prince Andrew, with whom, in the brilliant dreamlike extravagance of her first grand ball, she dances. Andrew is quite taken with her. He makes a bet with himself that if she goes in a certain order to certain people in the crowded ballroom, "she will be my wife." She does so. He is full of joy. Pierre, on the contrary, seeing his position for the first time with full accuracy for what it is-his wife almost public property, himself the "buffoon" - is dejected. In an exchange with him, Natasha urges upon him that it is a happy affair. She cannot imagine why he is sad - "such a capital fellow - For her the whole world is vibrating with love and joy.

CHAPTER TEN

The next day Andrew thinks briefly of the ball and Natasha, but dismisses both from his mind. Still he is ill-disposed to work. He loses interest in his reforming projects. How can they, he asks himself, "make me happier or better?" The vast amount of energy and time he has spent during his months in Petersburg has been spent, he decides, "on such useless work."

CHAPTER ELEVEN

Next day Andrew calls on the Rostovs. He is struck by their friendliness, good feeling, hospitality and naturalness. The contracts with the artificiality and coldness of all the ambitious people with whom he has been dealing is especially forceful. Natasha sings for them after dinner. He is filled with joy. That night he cannot sleep. "It did not enter his head that he was in love with Natasha ..." His only feeling is that he has been wasting his life on narrowing and unimportant affairs. "Pierre was right when he said one must believe in the possibility of happiness in order to be happy -" He concludes "let the dead bury their dead, but while one has life one must live and be happy."

Comment

Tolstoy's psychological analysis of the gradual growth of love in Andrew is masterly. Notice how it occurs, not in a general way, but specifically in the context of Andrew's unique, particular personality. Tolstoy takes Andrew's age, character, personality, and the determining factors of his life into account at all stages of development.

CHAPTER TWELVE

Berg, now married to Vera, invites Pierre and his wife to tea and supper. Helene has already refused the invitation; Berg is beneath her. Pierre promises to attend. Berg, who "measured his life not by years but by promotions," explains to Vera the system by which he works: be nice to people above one, and seek favors from them. Pierre arrives at the home of these two coldly ambitious persons first. Boris also attends, condescendingly. The Rostovs are also there. Pierre, at cards, is seated opposite Natasha, who has changed since the ball. She is more grave, gentle. "What's the matter with her?" thinks Pierre. Prince Andrew, also present, talks to her with a "look of tender solicitude." Pierre discerns that something important is occurring between these two. Vera, in her usual tactless way, tells Andrew of Natasha's youthful love for Boris, and implies that she is fickle. Andrew frowns and, disconcerted, moves off. Berg is happy, however; the party has been a success.

CHAPTER THIRTEEN

Andrew visits the Rostovs. It is obvious that he wishes to speak to Natasha. Left alone with her, he says nothing. When he leaves, Natasha and her mother talk: this is "the real thing." Andrew, later, consults with Pierre: he is in love with Natasha and resolved to make her his wife. Now it is Andrew who is ecstatic, while Pierre is gloomy, full of sadness, questioning life. "The brighter Prince Andrew's lot appeared to him, the gloomier seemed his own."

Comment

Now Pierre and Andrew are at opposite poles. Life, Tolstoy shows us, is full, large, various, changeful, inclusive.

CHAPTER FOURTEEN

Old prince Bolkonsky does not receive the news of Andrew's intended marriage gracefully. In fact, not liking anything which will upset the order of his existence, he insists on a year's postponement. Andrew returns from Bald Hills to Natasha in Petersburg. During his unannounced absence, Natasha has been filled with anxiety. When he returns, he goes immediately to the Rostovs and asks Natasha's hand in marriage. They will be married, following his father's condition, in a year.

CHAPTER FIFTEEN

Andrew visits the Rostovs as Natasha's fiancee. However, he must go abroad now. On the evening of his departure, he brings Pierre with him. He tells Sonya that if anything should happen to him or Natasha while he is away, she should seek Pierre's advice, for "he has a heart of gold."

CHAPTER SIXTEEN

This chapter is taken up with a long letter from Andrew's sister Mary to her friend, the heiress, Julie Karagina. Old Prince Bolkonsky has grown more and more irritable, domineering, angry. He is especially angered by Andrew's disregard of his wishes. Although Andrew is happier, more affectionate, his body is weaker, thinner, more nervous. The trip abroad was, in fact, a recommendation from his doctor. He is seeking a cure.

Comment

Up to this point the reader has not been told that Andrew is in ill health. Tolstoy's multiple points of view enable us to see now the import of Andrew's request to Sonya that should anything happen. Pierre must be consulted.

CHAPTER SEVENTEEN

Mary receives a letter from Andrew in Switzerland, where he is in a health resort. It is six months after his engagement. He asks Mary to seek a reduction in the number of months to his marriage from the old Prince.

Bolkonsky refuses; he threatens to marry Mary's companion, the Frenchwoman Bourinne and give Andrew "a step-mother." Mary resolves to become a pilgrim, one of "God's folk," but is unable to carry through her plan. She loves her father (in spite of his constant torment of her) and "little Koko," Andrew's son, too much. On this note of contrasting pride and humility, the old Bolkonsky's irritable unhappiness and the young Prince Bolkonsky's resignation and calm joy, Book Six comes to an end.

Comment

As Tolstoy promised the reader at the beginning of this Book, it has been about "real life." The years pass; we have seen "health and sickness, toil and rest, ----- intellectual interests in thought, science, poetry, music, love, friendship, hatred and passion." As we approach the halfway point of this immense work, we begin to see that Tolstoy's task is to survey all of existence, his goal to build a simulacrum of human existence, his subject humanity and those things that are humanity's expression of itself.

WAR AND PEACE

. . . .

BOOK SEVEN

CHAPTER ONE

The affairs of the Rostovs are anything but bright. Because of the Count's prodigality the family is in danger of becoming impoverished. The Countess urges Nicholas to return home from his regiment to handle their affairs. Home on leave, he wonders about the validity of Natasha's engagement to Prince Andrew.

CHAPTER TWO

Nicholas attempts to remedy the tangled affairs of the Rostovs and ends by kicking the estate's manager Mitsenka down the six steps of the main building. Later embarrassed, he realizes that he has made a mistake, and that he has no head at all for business. Giving it over, he devotes himself to hunting.

CHAPTER THREE

Nicholas goes on a wolf hunt. The serf Daniel prepares for the expedition. At the last moment Natasha insists on going along.

CHAPTER FOUR

The hunt begins. It is a gray, wet morning in autumn. On the move, the hunting party is joined by "Uncle," a neighbor and distant relative. Old Count Rostov, waiting in a convenient place for the wolf to appear, inopportunely lets him escape.

CHAPTER FIVE

The wolf is taken, however, alive.

CHAPTER SIX

The hunt continues, now for fox, later for hares. "Uncle's" dog is given credit for the catch.

CHAPTER SEVEN

Natasha and Nicholas are invited to spend the evening at his estate. He is by no means wealthy. Everything is clean but run down. The serfs are quite primitive. A feast of country food, magnificently prepared by "Uncle's" cook, is served. "Uncle" explains that this is how he is finishing his days: "Death will come - Nothing will remain. Then why harm anyone?" He has a wonderful reputation as a just man, always ready to help settle disputes; however, he refuses any kind of public appointment. Mitka, his coachman, plays the balalayka (a Russian, hand-held, stringed instrument, of the same family as the banjo and guitar). Natasha dances a Russian folk dance. Servants come to pick up Natasha and Nicholas.

Comment

These last six chapters form a group, bound together by the hunt. They have to do with the joys of simple country life. All the people are "good." They culminate in the visit to "Uncle," a man close to the soil, a man of justice and integrity. Leaving aside the last book, which is not properly part of the narrative, we find here the dead center of the grand arch of Tolstoy's narrative. Anyone who wishes to know what Tolstoy sees as the indisputably essential elements of the good life find them here. Going home, Natasha says, "I know that I shall never again be as happy and tranquil as I am now." Nor will she be until, in the course of suffering and indecision, she again attains with Pierre the simple pleasures of family life which she has known here.

CHAPTER EIGHT

The financial affairs of the Rostovs continue to grow worse. "The count moved in his affairs as in a huge net, trying not to believe that he was entangled but becoming more and more so at every step ... ." The countess sees only one way out: Nicholas must marry the wealthy heiress Julie Karagina, Princess Mary Bolkonskaya's friend. Nicholas, who has gone along for many years on the assumption that he will marry the impoverished Sonya, knows that he can be happy with her; still, he does not wish to sadden his parents. The matter is put off. A letter from Andrew informs the family that his old wound has reopened. "Things were not cheerful in the Rostov's house."

Comment

Note how quickly Natasha's prediction about her happiness comes true. Note too that Nicholas is in great measure responsible for his present predicament: the reader will recall the huge debt of 43,000 rubles his father had to pay to Dolokhov.

CHAPTER NINE

Christmas is celebrated - not a particularly joyous one. Nicholas must return to his regiment soon. Natasha cannot bear the absence of Andrew any longer; she acts strangely, giving orders and later countermanding them. Sick with longing, she grows bored and dissatisfied.

CHAPTER TEN

Nicholas, Natasha, and Sonya relive the past. Natasha has the feeling that life is over for her; she cannot imagine that she will ever be happy again. Still, recalling old events, she becomes wistfully gay once more. The house serfs, dressed up in outlandish costumes, come to amuse them with their antics and to play "Christmas games." The younger members of the family dress up and put on skits. Sonya's costume makes her particularly lively and attractive. They go out into the snow-filled night and drive off in sleighs. They begin to race each other along the frozen roads. They come, through the enchanted world to Melyukovka, a neighboring estate, and are met by maids and footmen with candles.

CHAPTER ELEVEN

Here, dressed all in incredible and imaginative costumes, they dance and entertain the owners. Refreshments are served. Sonya goes to the barn to try her fate. Nicholas cannot take his gaze from her. He intercepts her on the way to the barn and kisses her.

Comment

It was a superstition, local to the estate, that a young woman going to the barn alone would there learn her fate. In this case, it would appear, the superstition has some truth in it: Sonya learns that Nicholas loves her.

CHAPTER TWELVE

The party of Rostovs drives back home. Nicholas "felt himself-in fairyland." Arriving, he tells Natasha; she is happy. Later the young girls talk alone. They try to see into the future by looking into the mirror.

Comment

The use of the mirror to see into the future is, of course, another superstitious practice. Note here that the scene is used to suggest impending disaster. And to which of the lovers will disaster come: Sonya's or Natasha's?

CHAPTER THIRTEEN

Nicholas tells his mother of his love for Sonya and his desire to marry her. The countess opposes the match. She is cold. Nicholas does not recognize this aspect of his mother's character. There is a scene. A reconciliation between mother and son is effected. Nicholas returns to his regiment. The countess' health deteriorates. But Andrew is expected in Moscow. Leaving the countess behind, the old Count returns to Moscow. It is the end of January.

Comment

The reader will recognize how similar the ending of this Book is to the previous one. Then, Andrew's relationship with his father had broken down over the question of his marriage to Natasha; now, a year later, Nicholas' relationship with his mother has broken down over the question of his marriage to Sonya. Thus, Tolstoy shows us that life is both the same and different, that the great cycles of human existence bring up, generation upon generation, the same questions which must be answered, the same decisions which must be made.

WAR AND PEACE

. . . .

BOOK EIGHT

CHAPTER ONE

This Book will cover events of the years 1811–1812. We return to Pierre. More than ever before he questions the whole purpose of his life: "Only the skeleton of life remained" and "dull formalities." He returns to his life of drinking and carousing and leaves Petersburg for Moscow, where "he felt at peace-as in an old dressing gown." His heart and purse are so good, his intellect so benevolent, that he becomes a favorite. All his old plans and ambitions seem quite lost. But the worm of discontent still gnaws deeply in him. He drinks more, not out of amiability but necessity. He cannot find the answer to "it."

Comment

The reader is reminded that it was the crushing weight of this question which drove Tolstoy, some fifteen years later, to the verge of suicide.

CHAPTER TWO

Old Prince Bolkonsky and his daughter are also in Moscow. He has become quite senile, and even more doctrinaire and harsh in his senility. Mary suffers greatly; she is bound to her father, the victim of his irritability and tantrums.

CHAPTER THREE

The Prince is visited by a French doctor whom he takes for a spy and orders out of the house. It is the Prince's name day. A small group, including Pierre and Boris, is invited to celebrate. The talk is political. Relations with Napoleon, calm until now, are deteriorating. There will be a war.

CHAPTER FOUR

Mary and Pierre talk after the dinner is over, he noting that Boris is always about when there is a wealthy heiress to be courted, she inquiring about the personality of Natasha. Prince Andrew is expected very shortly; against her will she longs to think well of her future sister-in-law.

CHAPTER FIVE

The fortunes of Boris are followed. He is indeed courting all the wealthy heiresses. He has not been successful in attaining a good match in Petersburg; hence, he lays siege to Julie Karagina in Moscow. The latest fashion is to be melancholy; he is successfully melancholy with Julie. He proposes and is accepted.

Comment

The fashion for melancholy is the result of Romanticism which had now made its belated appearance in Russia. Early English Romanticism was nourished in part by the Graveyard School of poetry, so called for its addiction to the **theme** of death, the impermanence of life, and its fondness for setting poetic reflections on these **themes** in cemeteries. Jane Austen makes great fun of this fad among young people in her novel *Sense and Sensibility*.

CHAPTER SIX

The Rostovs return to Moscow. They stay at the home of Marya Dmitrievna "the terrible dragon" with whom the old Count, you will remember, had danced so enthusiastically.

CHAPTER SEVEN

Count Rostov takes Natasha to call on her future father-in-law, Prince Bolkonsky. The old Prince is ailing; Mary receives them and instantly finds that she cannot abide Natasha. In turn, the young girl out of pique at the offensive way in which they have been greeted, finds that she dislikes Mary. The visit turns out to be a dismal failure.

CHAPTER EIGHT

The Rostovs with Sonya attend the opera. Boris and Julie are in the audience, as is Dolokhov who has, continuing his mad escapades, recently returned from Persia, where, the rumor is, he had killed the Shah's brother. Sonya's "former adorer" and his friend, Anatole Kuragin, are the favorites of the Moscow ladies. Helene, Pierre's wife, who has followed him to Moscow, has the next box. She and Natasha evaluate each other's beauty.

Comment

Tolstoy, who loved music, attended the opera frequently. Note that here, for the first time, Pierre's present and future wives confront each other.

CHAPTER NINE

Anatole Kuragin sits with Dolokhov in his stall, saying rather loudly that Natasha is "charming." At the intermission Boris comes to invite them to his wedding. Later Pierre, bored, comes by to talk. Anatole visits his sister Helene in the adjacent box and leaves. Helene invites Natasha to sit with her.

CHAPTER TEN

Anatole returns to his sister's box and is introduced to Natasha. Anatole's attentions are so intense that Natasha feels embarrassed, as if she were doing something improper in talking to him at all. He invites her to a costume ball and leaves. Only later, after she has returned home, is she able to see the situation clearly and is horrified that she has betrayed Prince Andrew.

CHAPTER ELEVEN

This chapter is concerned with the affairs of Anatole and Dolokhov in Moscow. Dolokhov uses Anatole, who has a prominent position in society, to lure rich young men into his gambling set. Anatole does not see himself as a bad person. He is a "male magdalene" (after Mary Magdalene, the prostitute forgiven by Christ in the Gospel "because she has loved much");--------all will be forgiven him, for he enjoyed much.' Natasha has made a strong impression on him. He sets his sights, so to speak, on her.

CHAPTER TWELVE

Helene invites the Rostovs to a recital, telling Natasha that her brother is "madly" in love with her. Under the malignant influence of the amoral Helene, the situation looks quite different. If this attractive and radiant woman approves, how can there be anything wrong with seeing Anatole again. The invitation is accepted.

CHAPTER THIRTEEN

At Helene's reception Anatole pushes his campaign with Natasha. In a little room he takes her hand, declares his love, and kisses her passionately. At home she cannot sleep but is tormented by conflicting emotions; her love for Andrew, the irresistible attraction of Anatole. What if she loves both?

Comment

In the notes which he drew up before composing *War and Peace*, Tolstoy wrote that Natasha "needs a husband, even two," to indicate the great capacity for life she has. Here the thought occurs to her that all the great love of which she is capable may be too much for one man alone.

CHAPTER FOURTEEN

Natasha receives a letter from Mary, asking forgiveness. But Natasha, for whom things have changed, does not know what to reply. Then a letter from Anatole (composed by Dolokhov) arrives, a letter of great passion. "Yes, yes! I love him," thinks Natasha reading it.

CHAPTER FIFTEEN

Sonya finds Anatole's letter and, horrified, remonstrates with her friend. But Natasha will not be talked to; she is rapturously in love with Anatole, "his slave." After this, Natasha writes to Mary breaking off her engagement to Prince Andrew. Anatole, dishonorable in his intentions, gets Natasha to agree to elope. Sonya discerns this and resolves to prevent it. The Count is away on business. There is no one to turn to.

CHAPTER SIXTEEN

Anatole and Dolokhov have made plan for Natasha's "abduction." She is to meet him behind the Kuragin house and then they will drive to a small village where an illegal marriage will be performed.

Dolokhov warns him that it is a stupid affair; that it will go to the courts, where it will come out that Anatole is "already married."

CHAPTER SEVENTEEN

Natasha does not appear. Anatole and his friends drive to Mary's house, but are stopped by the gigantic footmen. Shouting "betrayed," Dolokhov pulls Anatole back into the troyka (an open carriage-sleigh).

CHAPTER EIGHTEEN

Sonya has told Marya Dmitrievna everything. "The terrible dragon," not wasting any time, has simply locked Natasha in her room. After Anatole has gone off, Marya speaks with Natasha, who sobs and cries with frustration and anger. Next day on her father's return, she remains in her room.

CHAPTER NINETEEN

Pierre visits Natasha; he has been avoiding her because "his feeling for her was stronger than a married man's should be for his friend's fiancee." Now, at Marya's bidding, he comes. He is informed of the whole affair. Pierre tells Natasha that Anatole is already secretly married.

CHAPTER TWENTY

Pierre seeks out Anatole, the blood rushing to his heart. Finally he finds him in his own home, where he is consulting with

Helene. He drags him off, the terrible rage of which he is capable showing in his face. Alone, Pierre upbraids him for his conduct and orders him to leave Moscow. The next day he does.

CHAPTER TWENTY-ONE

Natasha, almost deranged by grief at the outcome of the affair, tries to poison herself. The news of the attempted suicide is all over Moscow. Pierre awaits with dread Andrew's return, knowing how terrible the dishonor will be to him. Andrew, finally arriving, hears that Natasha has broken her engagement and of her attempted elopement at the same time. Andrew, in better health, takes it, on the surface, very well, but Pierre recognizes in Andrew's animation the same characteristic desire to suppress pain and grief and dishonor which he has noted in himself. He asks Pierre to return Natasha's portrait and letters, and requests that her name never be mentioned to him again.

CHAPTER TWENTY-TWO

Pierre fulfills his commission by visiting the Rostovs. Natasha asks to see him. She asks Pierre to beg Andrew's forgiveness for the wrong she has done him. She cries. Her life is over. Pierre says: "All over? If I were not myself, but the handsomest, cleverest, and best man in the world, and were free, I would this moment ask on my knees for your hand and your love." Natasha weeps tears of gratitude and leaves the room. Pierre now realizes he is in love; he has suppressed the feeling for Natasha for a long time. Now he is exhilarated. Driving home in the frosty night, he sees the great comet of 1812. "It seemed to Pierre that this comet fully responded to what was passing in his own softened and uplifted soul, now blossoming into a new life."

Comment

The reader will note here how the comet symbolizes for Pierre what the flowering oak symbolized for Andrew. He will note too how as Andrew's fortunes are depressed Pierre's are exalted, and vice versa. By these slow cycling of men's fortunes Tolstoy manages to convey the diversity of human existence, its changes, its flow its multiplicity. Life goes on, changing direction and depth: nothing ever remains the same. For Natasha, too, life will go on.

WAR AND PEACE

BOOK NINE

. . . .

CHAPTER ONE

It is the year 1812. Tolstoy interrupts his narrative, as he will now do from time to time, to analyze the elements of the historical process. The historians, he says, will give such and such reasons, as if the causes were to be located in the official documents. It is impossible to isolate one single cause or even a single group of causes. Innumerable causes combine to bring an event about; the war "had to occur because it had to. Millions of men, renouncing their human feelings and reason, had to go from west to east to slay their fellows, just as some centuries previously hordes of men had come from east to west slaying their fellows." It is finally impossible to explain great events fully. They are precipitated by such multitudes of pressures and counter-pressures that the total can only be described as "the ferment of the people."

CHAPTER TWO

Napoleon, joined by the Poles, crosses the Niemen River into the territory of Russia. Crossing the swift flowing Viliya River further into Russian territory, some troops are drowned. Napoleon is simply pleased at their enthusiasm in attempting to swim the river rather than wait for a pontoon bridge to be built. He is sublimely egotistical. He imagines that he is personally the cause of it all.

CHAPTER THREE

Emperor Alexander reviews his troops. None seriously believe that a war is at the doorstep. It comes as a great shock to learn that Napoleon has already begun his invasion of Russian soil. Boris, moving higher up the ladder of society, actually overhears the Emperor receiving the news. Alexander writes to Napoleon, offering to ignore the invasion if the French Emperor will withdraw.

CHAPTER FOUR

Balashev, the Adjutant General who had given the news to Alexander, is dispatched to Napoleon with the Tsar's letter. Meeting the French invaders, he is treated with a rudeness to which he is not accustomed. On his way to see Napoleon, he meets Murat, Napoleon's general who is addressed as "King of Naples." He wishes Balashev success in his mission.

CHAPTER FIVE

Next Balashev is taken to Davout, Napoleon's Marshal, a cruel, nasty, impetuous person. He treats Balashev with scant respect. He demands the letter, but Balashev refuses to deliver it up to any but Napoleon. However, he is forced to give it up. After four days he is informed that Napoleon will grant him an audience.

CHAPTER SIX

Napoleon receives Balashev in a setting of great magnificence. The French Emperor is only interested in what takes place "within his own mind." He is Tolstoy's supreme egotist. He interrupts Balashev, systematically destroys any possible hope for peace. There is nothing to be done. He will send a letter to Alexander, whose "lofty qualities" he esteems. Balashev is dismissed.

Comment

We have seen innumerable examples of Tolstoy's "bad" people (Helene, Boris, Berg, Anatole) - self-seekers, egoists, immoralists - who have no conception that anything is important except their own desires. Napoleon is the arch egotist; like Satan, locked in the ice of Dante's hell, he is locked in the ice of his own self-importance; like Satan, he is evil because he will serve no other cause but his own desire.

CHAPTER SEVEN

Napoleon invites Balashev to dine with him. Paradoxically, he treats the Russian envoy as if he agreed with all his plans and purposes. So complete is his egoism. Balashev is dispatched with Napoleon's letter to Alexander.

CHAPTER EIGHT

Andrew, after his conversation with Pierre, had left Moscow and gone to Petersburg looking for Anatole. There Kutuzov, the Russian Commander, suggests that Andrew join him, as before, in his headquarters staff in Turkey, a country with whom Russia had an alliance. Life has become dull for him, the old vaulting sky which so inspired him once is low and oppressive. His dishonor rankles. He asks for a transfer to the Western Army. On his way there he stops off at Bald Hills. His father is irritable and orders him out. Mary urges him to be strong and endure suffering, to forgive Anatole. Half convinced, he departs, not having said good-bye to his father.

CHAPTER NINE

Andrew joins the army at Drissa in western Russia, in the so-called "Polish provinces." Andrew rides through the entire area familiarizing himself with the distribution of his troops. There is an analysis of the many plans offered to meet the invaders.

Comment

As he often does when dealing with large and complex settings, Tolstoy has one of his characters move through the area acting, in a sense, as a pointer or guide. The reader will recall how both Andrew and Nicholas Rostov served this purpose before and during the battle of Austerlitz. Of course, the end effect of this technique is to acquaint the reader with the situation.

CHAPTER TEN

Prince Andrew is called to the Emperor Alexander for an interview about conditions in Turkey. Here he meets Pfuel, "a German theorist," one of Alexander's generals. There is to be an informal council of war.

CHAPTER ELEVEN

The council of war continues. Various points of view are heard, various plains, various theories. Pfuel is dogmatic; he knows precisely what will occur, good and bad. Absolutely certain, he smiles aloofly, makes sarcastic rejoinders to the criticisms of his fellow generals. Those who do not agree with him are blunderers, stupid persons who do not know the "science" of war.

Comment

Tolstoy, as usual, is absolutely ruthless with the tacticians of the war. Generals, like kings, are "history's slaves" and not, as they think, its masters. Special disgust is always reserved for the Germans, whom Tolstoy regarded as pedantic and arrogant, and, hence, absurd. He was especially hard on them because of their tendency to engage in abstract reasoning about human affairs. His opposing point of view, of course, is that human affairs cannot be viewed dogmatically for the simple reason that life is essentially unpredictable.

CHAPTER TWELVE

Nicholas Rostov, with his regiment, receives a letter from his parents requesting him to retire and return home. He refuses. To Sonya he writes that when the war is over, he shall never be separated from her again. He is promoted to captain. The regiment, having been sent to Poland, retreats under orders, destroying whatever provisions they cannot carry with them. They camp in a field of rye in heavy rain. Here we meet Ilyin, a young officer who stands in the same relation to Nicholas as Nicholas once stood to Densov. Together they go to a nearby tavern where Mary

Hendrikhovna, the pretty German wife of the regimental doctor, is to be found with her husband, who is asleep.

CHAPTER THIRTEEN

In the general mood of happiness all the officers assemble in the tavern court to toast and praise Mary. She blushes joyfully. The doctor wakes and morosely asks her to go to their traveling cart.

CHAPTER FOURTEEN

Next day before the sun is up, the hussars move out, led by Nicholas, to meet the enemy. Nicholas no longer feels fear on going into action. He has "learned how to manage its thoughts when in danger." Soon, the guns can be heard ahead. Then on a hill overlooking the battle that's already going on, the hussars are lined up in preparation for a charge.

CHAPTER FIFTEEN

The French have driven back mounted troops already sent against them. Nicholas sees that if he attacks now he can overwhelm the enemy. Touching his horse's flanks, raising his glittering sabre, he orders a charge. On his fast Cossack horse, he overtakes the French officer he has selected, strikes him with his sabre, and knocks him to the ground. The officer, agonized, expecting death, looks up at him. All Nicholas' animation vanishes; the face of the enemy is "ordinary, homelike." He is taken prisoner. Later Nicholas is commended for the fine charge. Curiously he is not happy; the memory of the Frenchman's face upset him. On the strength of his good work, however, he is put in charge of a hussar battalion.

CHAPTER SIXTEEN

The narrative returns to the Rostovs. Natasha's illness has gotten serious. In pity for her condition, she is no longer blamed for the disgraceful affair with Anatole. She is cared for by the entire family; expensive doctors are in constant attendance. In spite of all their attentions, "youth prevailed" and Natasha begins to recover.

Comment

Tolstoy had a lifelong aversion to doctors and lawyers. In this work he always treats them with great sarcasm.

CHAPTER SEVENTEEN

Natasha continues her recovery. Her spirits however are still low. Her old dynamism is gone; an unaccustomed sadness marks her personality. "There was not joy in life, yet life was passing." She is glad to see only one person, Pierre. She is grateful for his tenderness, kindness, and delicacy of insight into her pain; she has no stronger feeling than that. In church, which she now attends with devotion, she feels the possibilities of renewal.

CHAPTER EIGHTEEN

At Mass on Sunday, Natasha prays that she may be taught to do good "forever, forever." The priest prays for the salvation of Russia, and offers special prayers for victory over Napoleon. Natasha, deeply moved, asks God to forgive all men their errors and faults, her too, and give them peace and happiness. She feels that God has heard her prayers.

CHAPTER NINETEEN

Pierre's whole attitude to life has been altered by the tender feeling he has for Natasha. In Petersburg and Moscow the news is that Napoleon has promised to be in both cities by autumn. He thinks of joining the army but does not. He has the feeling, for which he cannot account, that destiny has called upon him to defeat Napoleon. He will, therefore, await destiny's call.

CHAPTER TWENTY

At the Rostovs we find that Natasha's depression has left her; the outward sign of this is that she can now sing once more. Sonya reads Alexander's manifesto calling upon all Russians to take up arms and crush the invader. Petya, the youngest Rostov son, declares he will enter the army. Natasha realizes, for the first time, that Pierre loves her. Knowing that she knows, he resolves to stay away from the Rostov house.

CHAPTER TWENTY-ONE

The Emperor is in Moscow to stir up the people. Petya goes to the Kremlin to see him and to explain to him that he wishes to serve his country but that his parents will not permit him to. The crush of visitors and onlookers is terrible. Petya worms his way through the dense throng, is knocked aside, and briefly loses consciousness. The people grow hysterical calling upon the Emperor, "Father! Angel! Dear one!" The Emperor, dining, is urged to show himself to the people. He does so; a piece of biscuit which he is still holding falls from his hand to the pavement. The people rush to take it. Seeing this, the Emperor begins to toss biscuits to the crowd. Petya, to his intense joy, secures one.

Next day, his father arranges for him to serve where there will be least danger.

CHAPTER TWENTY-TWO

A group of Moscow gentry and merchants assemble to discuss Alexander's manifesto. Pierre, who is present, listens to some criticism of the conscription. It is a time for action, not discussion. The meeting ends with the uproar of conflicting voices.

CHAPTER TWENTY-THREE

The Moscow gentry offer the Emperor all they have to repulse the enemy. Filled with devotion, fired by his Emperor's presence, Pierre offers to supply and maintain a thousand men.

Comment

By ending this Book in the setting of Moscow, Tolstoy is able to show the reader the mounting excitement of the whole Russian people. In the scene below the Emperor's balcony at the Kremlin, people of all classes mingle, merge, become one. It is the whole people, energized by the desire to repulse Napoleon, who will defeat him, not the theorists, the planners, or the strategists. Now Tolstoy begins to mount to his **epic theme**, the unity and identity of the Russian people finding itself under the terrible pressures of invasion, war, rapine, desolation, and devastation.

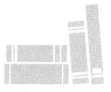

WAR AND PEACE

. . . .

BOOK TEN

CHAPTER ONE

The first chapter of this book is an analysis of the first stages of the campaign of 1812. The author's contention that the course of events is out of the hands of the planners (a fortuitous fact) is again advanced. It was the unforeseen abandonment and destruction of the great city of Smolensk by its own inhabitants which, more than anything else, inflamed the hearts of the Russian people with hatred of the invaders.

CHAPTER TWO

The narrative continues. At Bald Hills, Prince Bolkonsky blames Mary for his quarrel with Andrew, who has gone off without saying good-bye. He breaks relations with Mademoiselle Bourinne, the Frenchwoman whom he had threatened to marry. Julie Karagina, Mary's friend, writes her in Russian because she detests all that is French. "God's Folk," Mary's pilgrims, identify Napoleon with the anti-Christ. In a letter, Prince Andrew, who has begged and received his father's forgiveness, urges them to leave Bald Hills, which is in the line of retreat. The old Prince, obviously senile, does not grasp the meaning of the letter. The rest of the family sees that he is losing his grip on reality.

CHAPTER THREE

Prince Bolkonsky, in bed, reads the letter again and finally realizes the extent of Napoleon's invasion. He longs for death.

CHAPTER FOUR

Alpatych, a servant of Bolkonsky, is sent to Smolensk with a letter to the governor. Firing can already be heard in the outlying districts. The governor advises that Bald Hills be abandoned. The streets of the city are jammed with the wagons of those escaping with their household goods. Then the city is actually bombarded. Alpatych prepares a hasty departure. At dusk, the glow of the burning city illuminates the sky. In the retreating mass of soldiers who choke the streets, Alpatych is hailed by a familiar voice. It is Andrew. Hastily he directs Alpatych to get the Bald Hills and get the family to Moscow.

CHAPTER FIVE

In the retreat from Smolensk, Andrew passes Bald Hills with his regiment. he rides over to the now abandoned house. Everything is in disorder. Only Alpatych still remains with his family. Returning to his regiment, he finds that they are all bathing in a scummy pond trying to escape the terrible heat of the sun. Seeing all their healthy, naked bodies Andrew thinks, "flesh, bodies, cannon fodder!"

CHAPTER SIX

In Moscow, the rival salons of Anna Sherer and Helene are contrasted: Anna's has rejected the French, Helene's taken the position that Napoleon is a "great man" and seeks to excuse the war. Prince Kuragin, hurrying from one salon to another, sometimes grows confused and voices the wrong opinions. He, however, shares society's contempt for Kutuzov until he is appointed commander-in-chief. Then, Kuragin hastily reverses his opinion.

Comment

Kutuzov, old, blind in one eye, had been recalled to service upon Napoleon's invasion. He is, of course, Tolstoy's chief example of the man who understands the historical process, who waits for his opportunity and takes it. If there is a "hero" in the novel, it is Kutuzov.

CHAPTER SEVEN

The French draw nearer to Moscow. Napoleon questions Lavushka, Nicholas Rostov's Cossack orderly, who has been captured. Because he has gratified Napoleon's ego, the wily serf is set free and hastily returns to his master. Napoleon dreams only of capturing Moscow.

Comment

This incident of the interview with a captured Cossack, as is much else in the "public" portion of the narrative, is drawn by Tolstoy from the historians, in this case Thiers, a French historian. Note the way in which such material is incorporated into the texture of the novel. It is impossible to say what Tolstoy's incredible imagination invented, what the historical record gave him.

CHAPTER EIGHT

Old Prince Bolkonsky suffers a stroke and is paralyzed down the right side. He cannot speak. Then, barely able to speak, he begs Mary's forgiveness for all his cruelty to her. He dies.

CHAPTER NINE

This chapter is devoted to an analysis of the peasant character. Prince Andrew's peasants refuse to move away. It is rumored that they are in fact in contact with the French. They refuse to provide carts for the removal of the Prince's belongings.

Comment

Tolstoy, during the period of his religious crisis years later, devoted much of his time to the problems of poverty and ignorance among the people. Gradually he came to realize the great instability of a society filled with such horrifying inequalities, and clearly foresaw the Revolution of 1917. His prediction of it may be found in the book he published in 1886, *What Then Must We Do?*

CHAPTER TEN

Mlle. Bourinne advises Mary to seek protection from the French. Mary is horrified by the suggestion. At Andrew's estate, she orders all the grain distributed to the peasants.

CHAPTER ELEVEN

Mary assembles Andrew's peasants, urging them to take everything and go. They, however, distrust her and refuse to go. She orders preparations for her own departure in the morning.

CHAPTER TWELVE

At night Mary cannot sleep. She recalls in detail her father's last moments. She runs from the house in terror when he seems to appear before her.

CHAPTER THIRTEEN

Nicholas Rostov and his protege Ilyin, camped not far from Andrew's estate, go riding and come upon the house. Alpatych begs Nicholas to protect Princess Mary whom he does not know. Meeting her here, helpless, a virtual prisoner of the boorish peasants, strikes him as "a romantic event." He pities her. He offers her all his protection.

Comment

In this meeting, the last of the major characters are brought together. Nicholas and Mary who, the reader will remember, are based on Tolstoy's own parents, will find happiness with each other.

CHAPTER FOURTEEN

Nicholas upbraids the rowdy peasants and cows them. They disperse. They help to pack the carts. Nicholas escorts her part of the way and kisses her hand, denying any heroism on his part. Alone, Mary thinks that she has fallen in love with him. With his regiment, Nicholas considers the prospect of marriage to this wealthy heiress but, what to do about Sonya?

CHAPTER FIFTEEN

Prince Andrew's narrative is now taken up. Kutuzov has ordered him to report to headquarters. There he meets Denisov (of the lisp) who has recovered from his wound. Andrew recalls him as Natasha's first serious suitor. Denisov has a plan he wishes to present to Kutuzov - "guewilla warfare" (guerilla warfare). Kutuzov, as usual, is bored with all the elaborate plans offered him. He relies upon instinct.

CHAPTER SIXTEEN

Andrew is offered a place on Kutuzov's staff, an offer he declines, preferring to stay with his regiment. Kutuzov advises "patience and time." Andrew has great faith in Kutuzov because the old general "understands that there is something stronger and more important than his own will ..."

CHAPTER SEVENTEEN

In Moscow, after the ardor aroused by the Emperor's visit has died down, it is difficult to realize that there is great danger. In fact, at the approach of Napoleon's forces the people yield to a strange hilarity. Boris' wife Julie, preparing to leave Moscow, gives a farewell reception. Pierre attends. The affairs of the Rostovs are discussed. Little Petya is in the regiment which Pierre has formed. Pierre is told that Andrew's sister, Mary, is in Moscow.

CHAPTER EIGHTEEN

In his home, Pierre's cousin Catiche wishes to leave Moscow. Pierre will not hear of it. He goes to watch a balloon ascent, observes the public flogging of a Frenchwoman accused of being a spy. He cannot stand Moscow. He goes off to join the army.

CHAPTER NINETEEN

Tolstoy analyzes the battle of Borodino, which was effective in leading both to the destruction of Moscow and the depletion of Napoleon's army, bringing good neither to one side nor the other. Reason cannot account for the battle; the whole business was the result of accidents.

CHAPTER TWENTY

Pierre, seeking the "position" of the army, encounters advancing cavalry and wagons full of wounded soldiers. He goes to observe the digging of the entrenchments preparatory to the battle.

CHAPTER TWENTY-ONE

On the hillside Pierre surveys the scene. A procession, in which a holy relic of the destroyed Smolensk is carried among the troops, shows Kutuzov's deep piety.

Comment

Here, as is usual before a battle, Tolstoy shows the terrain and placement of the troops in the landscape through the eyes of one of his characters, in this case Pierre.

CHAPTER TWENTY-TWO

Pierre meets Boris, who shows him the camp. They make their way to Kutuzov, who notices Pierre and calls to him. Before Pierre can approach, his old dueling **protagonist**, Dolokhov, gets to Kutuzov; degraded in rank again, he is attempting to restore himself to favor. Kutuzov turns to Pierre and offers him the hospitality of the camp. Dolokhov begs Pierre's forgiveness. He is given it. Boris offers to show Pierre the line of troops: "it will interest you."

CHAPTER TWENTY-THREE

Pierre is shown the disposition of the troops. He does not understand the explanations given as to why they are so placed.

CHAPTER TWENTY-FOUR

Prince Andrew reflects on life and death, as he had done seven years before at Austerlitz. Now, however, the glory he once sought is totally meaningless to him. All will be swept away by death. Pierre, stumbling in, intrudes on his thoughts; the old friends greet each other restrainedly. Andrew cannot abide being reminded of his dishonor.

CHAPTER TWENTY-FIVE

Andrew explains the character of the war to Pierre; it is unlike any other war fought within memory, for now the Russians are fighting for their homeland. Pierre deeply understands this. War, says Andrew, is a terrible evil; it is murder, it cannot be justified. With premonitions of death, Andrew bids Pierre farewell. In his shed, he recalls his love for Natasha and his old pain is renewed.

CHAPTER TWENTY-SIX

Napoleon issues a proclamation - "short and energetic" - to his army.

Comment

Tolstoy shows us here some hint that for the first time Napoleon does not feel himself total master of the situation. He had, in fact, offered peace after the destruction of Smolensk.

CHAPTER TWENTY-SEVEN

Napoleon plans the disposition of his troops before Borodino. These plans are not carried out.

CHAPTER TWENTY-EIGHT

Historians say that Napoleon did not win the battle of Borodino because he had a cold. No, his will had nothing to do with it. It was the way the soldiers on both sides fought which brought about the results.

CHAPTER TWENTY-NINE

"The chessmen are set up, the game will begin tomorrow," says Napoleon, and this remark sums up his whole philosophy of life. At half-past five next morning, the first shots are fired. The "game" has begun.

CHAPTER THIRTY

Pierre views the battle from a hillside. The landscape is spellbinding. It is in terrible contrast to the smoke, death, noise, confusion, and carnage.

CHAPTER THIRTY-ONE

Pierre goes down into the battlefield. At a bridge his horse is wounded under him. All is terror, death, destruction. The group in which he finds himself is short of ammunition. Wagon loads of ammunition are blown up. He is in the way.

Comment

The battle of Borodino went on for ten hours. Note how Tolstoy indicates the passage of the hours.

CHAPTER THIRTY-TWO

The battery with which Pierre has found himself is captured by the French. Pierre attacks a French officer and escapes. The Russians recapture the battery.

CHAPTER THIRTY-THREE

The battle continues. It is impossible to know what is going on. Events take their own course.

CHAPTER THIRTY-FOUR

Napoleon cannot effect a victory. Even knowing this he allows the battle to go on. But it has ceased to be a battle: "it was a continuous slaughter which could be of no avail either to the French or the Russians."

CHAPTER THIRTY-FIVE

In Kutuzov's army, there is no thought of retreat. The old commander writes out the orders of the day for tomorrow: they will attack. The army is "comforted" by these words.

CHAPTER THIRTY-SIX

Prince Andrew is hit by a shell. He is taken to a dressing station.

CHAPTER THIRTY-SEVEN

On the operating table Andrew observes the wounded. It is the same flesh, he thinks, as that of the joyfully swimming soldiers. On the table next to him, having his leg amputated, is his old enemy Anatole. In spite of his own terrible wounds, he pities Anatole. He realizes that he has now found what he has been seeking, love of all mankind. "But now it is too late."

CHAPTER THIRTY-EIGHT

Napoleon is depressed by the terrible slaughter on the battlefield. He cannot make the Russians retreat no matter how much gunfire he concentrates upon them. But his conscience is not troubled by the deaths of fifty thousand men.

CHAPTER THIRTY-NINE

At the end of the day the battle ceases. Perhaps one slight effort on either side would have made victory decisive: the effort was not made. The Russians have lost an incredible one half of their army and have held.

Comment

The battle of Borodino is the decisive one for Tolstoy. The French here, he maintained, were mortally wounded and it was only the momentum of the invasion which carried them on to Moscow. The reader will note the sense of completion which repeated patterns give: just as at the battle of Austerlitz, Andrew has again been wounded. We do not know his fate. Contrast Napoleon after the battle of Austerlitz and after the battle of Borodino.

WAR AND PEACE

. . . .

BOOK ELEVEN

CHAPTER ONE

In this chapter Tolstoy continues his explanation of his historical method. Man can only understand laws of motion by selecting arbitrarily some elements of that motion. However this leads to human error, as is illustrated by the paradox of Achilles and the tortoise (in which by continuously dividing the distance he must cover before he reaches the tortoise, it is demonstrated that Achilles will never catch the tortoise; this is of course absurd). The same is true of an historical method which concentrates on arbitrarily chosen, discrete elements, instead of the continuous flow of humanity. Therefore, to truly understand history we must ignore kings, ministers, generals, and the like, and concentrate on what moves the people.

CHAPTER TWO

The Russian army falls back after Borodino to Moscow; the French army, within sight of its goal, Moscow, continues forward.

CHAPTER THREE

Kutuzov, at Fili, less than four miles from Moscow, holds a council of war. As usual, a multiplicity of contradictory plans is offered. Count Rostopchin comes from Moscow to join them. Kutuzov orders a retreat beyond Moscow; it is his task to save the army, to save Russia, not Moscow.

CHAPTER FOUR

The abandonment and burning of Moscow was inevitable, says Tolstoy; it was fated. The Russians simply could not, would not, accept French rule. This abandonment and burning was "the great work which saved Russia."

CHAPTER FIVE

Pierre's wife, Helene, returns to Petersburg. To two men, with whom she has an attachment, she indicates that perhaps there is a possibility of her remarrying. To accomplish this she becomes a Catholic, hoping that her first marriage to Pierre will be regarded as invalid and not binding in Rome. Her letter of intention is delivered to Pierre's house in Moscow when he is on the field of Borodino.

Comment

Helene, like Napoleon, assumes that everything is ordered to her own desires. Like Napoleon, she never doubts that whatever she decides is totally correct: paradoxically, it is this complete egoism which is the source of her strength.

CHAPTER SIX

We return to Pierre. After Borodino, he returns to the little town of Mozhaysk where, in the inn, he dreams. It seems in his dream that a voice speaks to him: he must "harness" all his ideas. Outside his window the groom is calling, "it is time to harness."

Comment

Tolstoy makes use here of the curious fact that accidental outside stimuli often supply apparently logical elements in one's dreams; this seems to be especially true just before one wakes. Pierre returns to Moscow.

CHAPTER SEVEN

In Moscow, Pierre meets Rostopchin who advises him to break off his relationship with the Masons, who are considered traitors, and to leave Moscow. Reaching home, he reads Helene's letter, falls asleep, and early next morning leaves him, no one knows whither.

CHAPTER EIGHT

The Rostovs prepare to leave Moscow. The Countess dreams of her two sons, Nicholas and Petya, being killed in battle. When Petya, in Pierre's regiment, returns, he is offended by her matronly attention. Sonya is sad because of Nicholas' obvious interest in Mary Bolkonskaya; he details his meeting with her in a letter. The house is opened to the wounded, who are arriving in thousands from Borodino. Natasha directs the packing. Another wounded man is brought in. It is Andrew! Preparations go on for the departure. Moscow citizens riot and loot. Berg, the Rostov's son-in-law, now a colonel, visits them. The wounded are placed in the carts, from which the trunks and household furniture have been removed. The family starts off. Natasha still does not know that Andrew is among the wounded that are going with them. On the way out of Moscow Natasha sees Pierre, disguised in a coachman's coat. He acts oddly, and says a hasty good-bye.

CHAPTER NINE

Pierre has, in fact, been living in Bazdeev's house, sorting his books. Bazdeev, the Freemason who had approached Pierre in the inn so long ago, had died.

CHAPTER TEN

Napoleon surveys Moscow from the hills surrounding it. He sends a deputation to Moscow to say that he will rule benevolently. But Moscow is empty. The signal is given to enter the city.

CHAPTER ELEVEN

In an elaborate **epic simile**, Tolstoy compares Moscow to a queenless hive of honey bees. Only a few drones circle aimlessly about.

CHAPTER TWELVE

The narrative doubles back in time to concentrate on Rostopchin, the governor of Moscow, and his actions before the city was abandoned. He has delivered up a young agitator to the mob which beats him to death. He leaves to join Kutuzov.

CHAPTER THIRTEEN

The French enter Moscow. There is no one to defend it. The troops lose their discipline looting the empty town. Moscow burns. No one is to blame: neither Rostopchin's patriotism nor the barbarity of the French. It was set on fire "by the soldiers' pipes, kitchens, and campfires ..."

CHAPTER FOURTEEN

Pierre, still in Moscow, forms a plan to kill Napoleon. He saves a French officer's life and becomes involved with him because of the officer's gratitude. They tell each other the story of their lives and loves.

CHAPTER FIFTEEN

The Rostovs, because of the congested roads, have not gotten too far from Moscow. At night they see the glow of Moscow burning. Natasha, who knows from Sonya that Andrew is wounded, is morose all day. At night, she resolves to see him and slips out. Andrew, in delirium, recognizes Natasha. "I love you more, better than before," says Andrew. They are reconciled.

CHAPTER SIXTEEN

Pierre, his intention to kill Napoleon as strong as ever, sets out to perform his task. He wanders through Moscow; he saves a child, defends an Armenian girl against a French soldier. Later he is arrested as an incendiary. He is placed under strict guard.

Comment

During this whole Book, the central event is the destruction and occupation of the city of Moscow. Pierre, who has come to represent the best impulses of the Russian people, is the center and focus of the Book. The "buffoon" has come into his own.

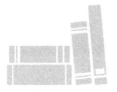

WAR AND PEACE

. . . .

BOOK TWELVE

CHAPTER ONE

In Petersburg, in spite of the occupation of Moscow, life goes on normally. At Anna Sherer's salon, we hear that Helene is ill. The news of the battle of Borodino arrives and there is great rejoicing. Unexpectedly, the news of Helene's death is announced. Official news has it that she died of an heart malady; rumor has it that she took an overdose of drugs because of unhappiness. Just after this, the fall of Moscow is announced. The Emperor Alexander resolves to fight on.

CHAPTER TWO

Nicholas is sent into the provinces to procure horses. He is the hit of the provincial society there, dances exuberantly, flirts with all the ladies, and generally has a fine time for himself. An old aunt of Mary Bolkonskaya is there. Her friend, the governor's wife, who knows Nicholas's mother, offers to arrange a marriage between himself and Princess Mary. He tries to explain about Sonya. This is brushed aside. He agrees. He goes to see Mary.

Their mutual attraction deepens. However, he does not wish to act basely. Deeply troubled, he prays for enlightenment. Then a letter from Sonya arrives. She does not wish to be the cause of woe to the family which has been so good to her: she is releasing him from his promise. In the same chapter, returning to the Rostov's, we find that the old Countess has intimidated Sonya into sending the letter. Natasha continues to care for the wounded Andrew. Sonya realizes that if Andrew gets well and he and Natasha are married, that Nicholas cannot marry Andrew's sister Mary. For this reason she has written the letter.

Comment

According to the rules of the Russian Orthodox Church one could not marry a sister-in-law's or brother-in-law's sister or brother. Since Andrew's marriage to Natasha would make Mary his brother-in-law's sister, Nicholas could not marry Mary. Hence, he would be free to marry Sonya.

CHAPTER THREE

Pierre, under arrest by the French forces, is taken to a guardhouse, accused of arson. He is condemned to be executed. With five others he is led to a field. Two by two the prisoners are tied to posts, their heads bagged, and shot and dropped into freshly dug pits. Pierre's partner is led away-alone. Pierre is saved and sent to the prisoner-of-war barracks. He feels that the order of the universe has crumbled completely. Among the prisoners he meets a soldier, a small man, a peasant. He offers Pierre a potato to eat. This is Platon. He has absolute faith in God and His Providence. Later, when most of these experiences have lost their sharpness, Pierre recalls Platon, "who always remained in his mind a most vivid and precious memory and the personification of everything Russian, kindly, and round." He is a completely happy man, "an unfathomable, rounded, external personification of the spirit of simplicity and truth."

Comment

In Platon, Tolstoy gives the reader the "personification" of "simplicity and truth." Here he says, is what one should be to be happy: simple, loving, dependent on God, continuous with life itself, pure, "rounded," unegotistical, selfless. He will be for Pierre the symbol of what he hopes finally to attain.

CHAPTER FOUR

When Princess Mary hears from Nicholas that the wounded Andrew is with the Rostovs, she goes to him; with her go Mlle. Bourinne and little Nicholas, Andrew's son. Her love for Nicholas Rostov fills her with strength. Natasha and she, united by grief, cry together and visit Andrew. He is cold, detached, dying. He waits death calmly, without fear. He has penetrated into the "new principle of eternal love." Total love consumes him. He wishes to renounce earthly life. Quietly, peacefully, after a lifelong struggle to know the truth, Prince Andrew dies.

Comment

In this short Book, two of the major characters in the novel die and one just escapes death. Helene's death is announced among the gossip of the society where her only existence lay; we are given all the details of Andrew's death. Pierre comes near death and escapes to be met by Platon, almost an emissary of God for his salvation. It is appropriate that the great death of Moscow should be the background for the death of one hero. But out of the ashes springs new life. Pierre will now be the only hero.

WAR AND PEACE

BOOK THIRTEEN

. . . .

CHAPTER ONE

Tolstoy continues to analyze the causes of historical events, using as his subject the retreat and flanking movement of Kutuzov's army, which eventually put the Russians in a position to destroy the French army of Murat, Napoleon's commander. Tolstoy makes again his central point that circumstances and not the particular will of any one man or group of men brought the event about. The two armies, during the autumn months, do not meet; the French, "wounded" at Borodino, occupy Moscow and pillage it; the army of Kutuzov waits, nourishing its strength and courage, eager to fight, but restrained by Kutuzov, who is waiting, waiting for the right moment to strike. Eventually an attack is ordered, one which Kutuzov does not wish. Plans go awry. Only one regiment is in its proper place. But the French retreat and the battle is regarded as a victory.

Comment

It will seem to those who know battles only from historical text that Tolstoy gives no credit at all to human intelligence and its ability to plan. Within the context of the novel, however, as the great artist controls and directs his material according to his overriding **theme**, such criticism has no useful place. In Tolstoy's world, his observations and conclusions are justified by the evidence he gives.

CHAPTER TWO

Napoleon remains in Moscow, allowing the troops to plunder the city of its incalculable treasures until October, and then, instead of engaging Kutuzov, he retires along the devastated Smolensk road. Each of his acts, says Tolstoy, was calculated, although he did not know it, to destroy his army. In Moscow, all had been disorder. In spite of proclamations the inhabitants do not return; the fires continue, pillaging by the troops continues, robbery and civil disturbances continue. The discipline of the soldiers crumbled; the "army, like a herd of cattle run wild ... disintegrated and perished with each additional day it remained in Moscow." Fear sets in. All this had led Napoleon to quit Moscow.

CHAPTER THREE

Pierre, still in captivity, is dressed in discarded clothing, has lost his flabbiness, has a beard and mustache. His "former slackness ... was now replaced by an energetic readiness for action and resistance." Platon continues to be his happy, exuberant "round" self. Even in the midst of privation Pierre has found peace of mind. "He had sought it in philanthropy, in Freemasonry, in the dissipations of town life, in wine, in heroic feats of self-sacrifice, and in romantic love for Natasha; he had sought it by reasoning - and all these quests and experiments had failed him. And now without thinking about it he had found that peace and inner harmony only through the horror of death, through privation, and through what he recognized in Karataev (Platon)." When the French leave Moscow, the prisoners are brought out. They watch the thousands of troops, burdened down with loot, jamming the roads and bridges leading from the city. In the retreat the prisoners are treated harshly. That night Pierre, suddenly illuminated by the stupidity of the whole business, laughs aloud. "They took me and shut me up. They hold me captive. What, me? Me? My immortal soul? Ha-ha-ha! Ha-ha-ha! ..." Above him the winter sky glitters with stars to limitless distances.

Comment

The reader will be reminded of Andrew's insight, brought to him first by the sight of the grand, limitless, and continuing heavens, into the freedom that indifference to circumstances brings.

CHAPTER FOUR

At the Russian camp the news of Napoleon's departure from Moscow arrives. A detachment sent to check what was thought to be a French division finds the whole army of Napoleon at the city of Forminsk. The news is reported to Kutuzov, who cries and praises God. "Russia is saved." The Russian army is finally unleashed in all its hatred, energy, and eagerness to destroy the enemy. The French cannot recover, or take the initiative. Everywhere they are hounded, destroyed. They flee in confusion, without discipline. One third of the troops gone, fled, lost, wounded or dead, Napoleon retreats westward to Smolensk.

WAR AND PEACE

. . . .

BOOK FOURTEEN

CHAPTER ONE

Tolstoy analyzes the character of the Napoleonic war: it is unique. In all wars before it, the conquerors had won. The people had been subjugated; in this war, the opposite had occurred. " --- the French army had ceased to exist." The Napoleonic empire was destroyed. This happened because the Russian people, fighting for its life, for its integrity, and for its identity had turned upon the invaders, burned crops and villages. It was a national war, a people's war. Napoleon had used the correct "rapier"; but he had been met by a "cudgel." The "rules" of war did not apply here. Napoleon, the "chessman" of destruction, was beaten because his opponent did not play by "the rules."

CHAPTER TWO

The partisan or guerrilla war begins when the French enter Smolensk. The peasants and Cossacks kill off the enemy as they would mad dogs. "The irregulars destroyed the great army piecemeal." Denisov (of the lisp) is one of these irregulars as is Dolokhov. They hide out in the dense forests, watching the movements of the French. In a heavy, sodden rain they set out to attack. A young officer brings him a dispatch. It is Petya Rostov. He begs to stay with Denisov. Led by a peasant guide they come upon a French detachment, then settle down waiting to attack them. Petya gives a captured French drummer boy food. Dolokhov arrives. He wants exact information about the French and decides to ride over.

Petya begs to join him. In the dark, at the French encampment, Dolokhov, with his usual arrogance and bravery, identifies himself as a French officer to the sentinel, and, refusing to give the password, rides insolently by him. The two ride to the big bonfire where the French are gathered. Having gathered the information he wishes, he departs at a leisurely pace. Petya is ecstatic at such heroism. He returns alone to report to Denisov. He cannot sleep for excitement. He is "in a fairy kingdom where everything was possible." In the attack the next morning Petya, heedless of Denisov's warning, rushes impetuously forward. In the assault, without having landed one blow, he is shot through the head. Among the Russian prisoners released by Denisov and Dolokhov is Pierre.

Comment

In this brilliant recreation of the nature of partisan warfare, Tolstoy once again shows his absolute mastery over everything he touches. In Petya's fate he shows us the pathetic spectacle of a delightful, vigorous, sweet young life snuffed out. And here as the war grows more horrible in its savagery, he emphasizes again its waste and evilness.

CHAPTER THREE

The narrative doubles back to relate Pierre's journey among the prisoners and brings us back again to the moment of his rescue. Many of the prisoners had died. Platon, on the third day of the march, had fallen ill. The peasant relates a story to him about a merchant, falsely accused of murder, who forgives everyone and by this turns the actual murderer's heart. (This same story is retold by Tolstoy in the famous tale "God Sees the Truth but Waits.") The story affects Pierre deeply. Next day they move on. Platon, sick, is left behind. Pierre does not look around when the shot is fired. He knows that Platon is dead. That night, encamped, they are freed by the attack described in the previous chapter. After it, Dolokhov, who refuses to take prisoners, systematically executes a hundred at a time.

CHAPTER FOUR

His army in tatters, Napoleon retreats beyond Smolensk. The historians, in spite of his evil, which came to nothing praise him, by the standard of "grandness." "For us," says Tolstoy, "with the standard of good and evil given us by Christ, no human actions are incommensurable. And there is no greatness where simplicity, goodness, and truth are absent."

CHAPTER FIVE

Tolstoy analyzes the reasons why the French were not cut off by the Russians in their flight over the frontier. The answer, for all the complex explanations offered by the historians, is simple. The French fleeing, which every Russian desired-why then hinder their flight and incur more loss of lives? "The Russian army had to act like a whip to a running animal. And the experienced driver knew it was better to hold the whip raised as a menace than to strike the running animal on the head."

WAR AND PEACE

BOOK FIFTEEN

CHAPTER ONE

After the death of Andrew, both Natasha and Mary are grief stricken. "But pure and complete sorrow is as impossible as pure and complete joy." The cares of life intrude upon their silent sorrow and draw them out. Mary, now without father or brother, has greater demands put upon her and is the first to recover from her wound. Natasha continues to brood, alone in her room. It is in the depths of her grief that the news of Petya's death arrives. This brings her out of her depression. She must "take part in life." The Countess is in delirium. "Petya's death had torn from her half her life." But this restores Natasha to life. Mary and Natasha are drawn closely together, bound by sorrow. Both leave for Moscow now that the enemy has left.

CHAPTER TWO

Tolstoy continues to analyze Kutuzov's character and handling of the war. He had devoted all his powers not to slaying men but to saving them. "That simple, modest, and therefore truly great, figure could not be cast in the false mold of a European hero - the supposed ruler of men - that history has invented." He was great because he discerned and followed the currents of humanity.

CHAPTER THREE

Kutuzov thanks his troops for their valor and service. The victory is theirs. Various scenes of camp life and the conversation of the soldiers are given.

Comment

When he commanded a gun battery at Sevastopol, Tolstoy used to listen to his peasant soldiers talking as he wrote in the corner of the hut. Here he uses the dialogue to show the good spirits of the troops even in subzero weather, and their charity for a sick Frenchman who stumbles out of the woods.

CHAPTER FOUR

The remnants of Napoleon's forces are pursued. The other commanders have out of jealousy for Kutuzov carried out a campaign against him at the court. He is to be replaced. He realizes that his duty is over and accepts this resignedly. Almost immediately he begins to feel the weariness of old age come upon him; his health begins to fade. The Emperor Alexander arrives at the town of Vilna, where Kutuzov is quartered. Although he rewards him with the Order of St. George of the First Class, the Tsar is not satisfied with Kutuzov. He wishes to carry the war further, against Kutuzov's judgment. The power is taken from him and assumed by the Emperor. "Nothing remained for the representative of the national war but to die, and Kutuzov died."

Comment

What Tolstoy means by the last quoted sentence is that the Russian war was over; the European war against the Napoleonic empire was not. Another leader was required; Alexander was that leader.

CHAPTER FIVE

After being released, the full effects of his privations and hardships overcome Pierre and he is laid up for three months. He had seen the dead Petya, had heard of Andrew's death, of Helene's. But the sense of freedom which he had gained in captivity remains with him. He no longer questions life but accepts it, joyfully, humbly. "That search for an aim had simply been a search for God - , he had learned - that God is here and everywhere." He had learned this from the peasant Platon. His questions are all answered. This joy spreads to others. Even Catishe who is tending him finds that she is fond of him. Recovered, he sets off for Moscow; everything has taken on a new significance for him.

Tolstoy compares the recovery of Moscow to the reassembling of a scattered ant colony. Pierre stays in an annex of his house which had not been burned. Soon after arriving he hears that Andrew's sister Mary is in town. He goes to visit her. In the reception room there is another lady dressed in black whom he takes to be a companion. "Do you really not recognize her?" asks Mary, after Pierre has talked for some time. "When she smiled,

doubt was no longer possible, it was Natasha and he loved her."
For the first time Natasha tells of her last weeks with Andrew.
At dinner Pierre tells of his experiences, conscious of what an
impression his words are making on Natasha, wishing for her
approval. After Pierre is gone, the women talk of him. "Do you
know, Mary," says Natasha, "he has somehow grown so clean,
smooth, and fresh-as if he had come from a bath-Out of a moral
bath." That night he cannot think, trying to come to a decision.
Next day he goes to visit Natasha again. He stays so long that
the women exchange glances. Natasha says good night. Then
he tells Mary all. "- I have loved her and her alone all my life,
and I love her so that I cannot imagine life without her." Mary
promises to help him. "A joyful, unexpected frenzy, of which he
had thought himself incapable, possessed him." Mary questions
Natasha. "You love him?" "Yes," whispers Natasha. And so the
great novel ends.

Comment

It has not perhaps struck the reader until this last chapter of the
last book that aside from all its other majestic properties and
characteristics, *War and Peace* is one of the great love stories
of all literature. The great strands of existence are all drawn
together, the victory of love and life affirmed over death and
destruction, in Natasha's whispered "yes."

. . . .

CHAPTER ONE

Tolstoy, as if unable to let his world go from him, wrote two long epilogues, giving further analysis of the operations of its principles. He brings us to the year 1820. He contrasts again and more explicitly the characters of Napoleon the egoist and Alexander, who receiving all the power of Europe into his hands after the defeat of Napoleon, renounced it.

CHAPTER TWO

The destinies of the various characters we touched upon are revealed. Old Count Rostov dies after Pierre and Natasha marry. Nicholas, hearing the news, retires from the army. The estate he inherits is so deeply in debt, he is advised to decline accepting it. Not wishing to defame his father's memory, he accepts it. He asks Mary, whom he admires and who is wealthy, to marry him. He becomes an excellent estate manager and soon is out of debt. He prospers, the serfs say of him " - he was a real master." Sonya lives on the estate with them, "a sterile flower." There are children: "little Natasha," the father's pet. Pierre and Natasha visit.

CHAPTER THREE

By 1820, Natasha has three daughters and a son. She is matronly and happy. Her old animation has been replaced by a dignified serenity. The subject which engrosses all her attention is her family, and husband. Pierre continues his happy state. The two families live a joyful, happy, family-centered life. Pierre goes to Petersburg and on his return talks to Nicholas about the affairs of the government, which have grown worse. Groups of men, interested in reform, have gathered. The overthrow of the government is their aim. Pierre has joined the society. Nicholas insists upon loyalty to the government.

Comment

Tolstoy originally planned to do a novel on the so-called Decembrist movement to take over the government and institute liberal reforms. This movement was suppressed and its leaders exiled to Siberia. Early notes for the novel suggest that Pierre would be the hero in this abortive attempt. In seeking the fundamental conditions out of which this plot developed, Tolstoy was led to the subject of *War and Peace*.

CHAPTER FOUR

Young Nicholas, Andrew's now adolescent son, having heard Pierre and his uncle Nicholas talking, swears to himself to emulate Pierre and be famous. "Everyone shall know me, love me, and be delighted with me!" "Yes, I will do something with which even he (his dead father) would be satisfied ..."

Comment

Here then, is where Tolstoy finally takes leave of this characters. Life continues, young girls grow old, the vivacity and brilliance of young manhood settles into the regular rounds of life. The young, repeating the cycle, are full of fire and ambition, and, unaware of what lies before them, swear in the secrecy of their hearts to conquer the world - that world which each one does conquer, but never in the way he expects. The final point of *War and Peace* is made. Life cannot be suppressed: each one must test himself against existence and, hopefully, come to joy.

SECOND EPILOGUE

This whole last second epilogue is an essay, philosophic in intent, on the difficult subject of free will and necessity. In one sense it is not an essential part of the novel; in another sense, the novel is a demonstration of its principles. Briefly, in great and complex matters individual free will is an illusion; that which happens has to happen; God or necessity determine the great currents of affairs; even individual actions are of questionable determinacy; if one analyzes some choice which one regards as freely made, one will see that it was in fact not free; true freedom lies in recognizing that "God is here and everywhere." The reader will of course recognize how this applies to Pierre's whole narrative, his feeling constantly that he is taking part in a determined action, his finding freedom in finding God.

· ·

PIERRE

It is impossible to dislike Pierre. He is intelligent but simple, shy but intrepid, bumbling in society but infinitely delicate in personal relations. We know from the beginning that he is different from those around him: his illegitimate birth, his immense wealth, his great stature, his more than human strength, his gargantuan appetite, his search for the meaning of life, his indifference to material things, and even his spectacles and tendency to plumpness set him apart. His outstanding characteristics are simplicity of heart, lack of egoism, human charity. His impulse is to help humanity; he understands both Andrew's and Natasha's plight; he forgives Dolokhov, and even his wife Helene. This very simplicity aids him in ignoring the opinion society has of him as a buffoon. He understands more than any other character the fundamental requirement of life: to search for the truth, serve humanity, to live well. Because of his extraordinary qualities, he is the hero of the book. In his solution to life's problems we find Tolstoy's solution.

ANDREW

Like Pierre, Andrew is a searcher for the meaning of existence; unlike Pierre, his heart's impulse is checked by pride, cynicism, and intellect. Only in death does he reach a final solution. His ambition prompts him to excell, first in society, then in the army. His intelligence shows him that these are empty ambitions. He is as intellectual as Pierre is not; he questions life in a more systematic manner. His spirituality is not as spontaneous as Pierre's; it is perhaps more refined. Logical, brilliant, talented, his life is unhappy because he cannot merely exist from moment to moment, as does Platon, who is dependent on Providence, or like Anatole and Helene, who are in love with their egos. In his death, Tolstoy suggest that pure rationality, even though it discovers the truth, is insufficient, that the Andrews of the world will never be satisfied except in death.

NATASHA

Natasha is the heroine because of her unique combination of beautiful qualities: she is intensely loving, selfless, vital, womanly, natural, and gay. She loves music sports riding, dances, country pleasures, family life. She is competent, bears her pains and disappointments without despairing, learns from them, grows and adjusts. We watch her grow from an irresistible but slightly plain young girl to a stormy adolescent to a mature housewife and mother. In this last capacity she fulfills her destiny. Her need for love and to give love is so intense that it has led her into foolish situations: now finally, her love directed into proper channels, she quiets down and achieves peace.

PRINCE VASILI KURAGIN

This father of the corrupt Kuragin clan gives us insight into the cause of his children's bad characters. His eye always cocked for the main chance, he has no opinions but those which keep him safe with those in power. He is not immoral, so much as amoral. He does nothing because of ethical principles; he will never be found upholding an unpopular cause. He is a complete pragmatist; a chameleon whose ability to melt into the atmosphere of the particular situation he is in has enabled him to survive so long near the seat of power. Never in the eye of the camera, so to speak, he is always one of those in the background, the manipulator, the man to see if one wants something done. He places his children as if they were chesspieces, using them to gain, through marriage, more money, more land, more power. Life for him is a contest, a game, He takes subtle pleasure in coming out on top. His punishment is to see his children come to bad ends-Helene to an early death, Anatole the rake, deprived of a leg, Hippolyte all but an idiot. Still, he has, through so many years, played his artificial role that one cannot imagine him reacting to any of these tragedies in a normal, human way. Once only is the veil lifted: at the death of Count Bezukov. Pierre's father, his manipulations to deprive Pierre of his fortune, having come to naught, he betrays himself-death, he cries, will come to all. At heart, very deep, he realizes the absurdity of it all, but he cannot change his ways.

PRINCESS HELENE KURAGIN

She is extraordinarily beautiful. Her habitat is society. She is selfish and without moral values of any kind. An egotist, nothing has ever happened which might cause her to question herself. She has great animal force; believing so completely in herself, she carries the prizes of life off easily. But she has no interior life. She has never suffered. She has no spiritual life. She goes with the leader, because he is the leader. Her life had become completely public, like a great actress whose private existence is hard to imagine, she exists only in a certain setting, tapping a fan, making small talk, showing her marvelous shoulders, the envy and desire of all. Her death is tucked away in society conversation, between talk of balls past and balls to come.

PRINCE ANATOLE KURAGIN

Like his sister, handsome, full of unquestioning self-esteem, he preys on the ladies. A playboy and wastrel, he inevitably gets into trouble. Protected by his father's powerful influence at court, he is never disgraced. His whole life is one of self-satisfaction. He tries to carry off Natasha, not because he loves her but because he is jaded. He too has no interior life; he is completely without a sense of the spiritual life. Like the sons of many fathers who have devoted their entire energies to their own success in life, he is without direction, careless of the rights of others, in the end pitiful. His amputated leg is his end or his salvation. This tragedy will, we know, either destroy him-for he has no interior resources-or serve to start the process by which he will see himself for what he is and thus change.

DOLOKHOV

It is impossible to dislike Dolokov completely. His energy, bravery, cleverness in the fact of life are overwhelming. He is a great natural force. He has little respect for any other human being and fleeces the unwary without mercy. A ladies man, a wastrel, a gambler, a murderer, still he has barbaric attractiveness. He goes back to the primitive. Life for him is a jungle in which the clever, the brave, and the strong survive. He is the one who in a war wins citations and rises to command. In peace, one finds him in prison. He will not survive civilization unless he changes.

When the frontier is still growing he becomes a hero. Like the true primitive he is, he blubbers like a baby at the thought of hurting his poor old mother. Only his superior natural intelligence separates him from that type of dock walloper who when he rolls up his sleeve to crack his opponent on the jaw reveals tattooed across his muscle "Mother."

PRINCESS ANNA DRUBETSKYA

Anna is the mother who will suffer any affront to push her child, boy or girl, on the success. She lives for her own, Boris. Impoverished but undaunted, she pours into Boris from childhood on all her ideas of what success means. He is an apt pupil. Only she is a match for Prince Kuragin, as tough as he, as deft a manipulator. She stands for hours in the outer office waiting to see the director; ignored, treated with disrespect, she will not go away. Eventually one gives in to get her off one's back. One knows however that the successful Boris, having learned his lesson about being nice only to those who can help him, will eventually realize his mother can no longer be of service and have nothing to do with her. But off in the corner, as she grows older, she will watch as he rises up the ladder and smile contentedly. For in a sense that Boris will never recognize, he is herself. His success is hers.

BORIS DRUBETSKY

Boris has only one ambition in life: success. His creed is known only those who can aid you. Human relationships like love, friendship, respect are useful hooks by which one can climb toward the top. He uses people, as his mother has. Apparently sufficiently intelligent to make himself indispensable to those he serves, we know that as he grows older he will begin to resemble Prince Kuragin more and more. Like the Kuragins he has no spiritual life. But he will never, never offend the accepted social conventions, even if this means going to Church every Sunday. He is, as he grows older in the novel, less and less likeable.

COUNTESS NATALY ROSTOVA

Natasha's mother is full of love for the family. She wants her children's happiness. They seek her out as their confidant. She understands Natasha's nature, her great need for marriage, motherhood, domestic life. However, the old Countess understands the value of a dollar, especially since her good-natured husband is so profligate. When Nicholas wants to marry the poverty-stricken Sonya, she will have none of it. Eventually in Natasha's marriage to Pierre and Nicholas' to Mary, she sees her two surviving children situated as she had desired, with, of course, the family fortunes magnificently restored. Old age, after many hardships, comes to her with dignity.

COUNT ILYA ROSTOV

The old Count, full of love for his fellowman, cannot resist showing it by an over lavish hospitality. So great is his prodigality that he ruins the family estate bringing about the situation which denies to Nicholas marriage to Sonya. Rostov is not at all a practical man, but he does not waste things on himself. He is the loveable profligate who insists on picking up the check, keeping his house open, throwing parties for the least excuse. He loves people to enjoy themselves and beams when they do and he is the cause of it. Typically he has no head for business, cannot pay attention to details and leaves them to his managers, who in turn dip into his capacious pockets. Eventually, he shows an inability to survive disaster. After the terrible events of the war, he is no longer sure of himself, cannot revive the old spirit of gaiety which once pervaded him and dies.

COUNTESS VERA ROSTOVA

Natasha's older sister is a snip. She has excellent manners and follows the rules laid down for behaviour precisely, but no one really likes her. She is artificial and cold. Without exactly meaning to do so, she always says just the wrong thing. Her impulses do not come from the heart but from the book of etiquette. In Boris she finds a suitable match. As she grows older she will become a shrew, a precise, cold, unlovable woman who will do everything correctly but without spontaneity or warmth.

COUNT PETYA ROSTOV

Although he is about during the whole book, this young man does not come forward as a major character until his early teens and then only to die, cut down by a bullet in the raid which frees Pierre. He is the major symbol of the useless waste of war. Full of romantic notions about the glory of battle, he rides to his pitiful death without so much as throwing a stone against the enemy.

SONYA

Poor, orphaned, dependent on the goodness of her relatives the Rostovs, Sonya has had the impulse for self-fulfillment pulled from her by circumstances. Loving, thoughtful, kind, practical, she knows her place. She has always loved Nicholas and for him turns down her one offer of a match with Dolokhov. Eventually she takes her place in Nicholas's household, "an unfertilized flower." She is almost defective in her lack of self-will. From birth to death she will exist as one who carries out the will of others. She has no life which is not an expression of her desire to serve others. This is, one feels, thrust upon her and not something that goes against her character.

PRINCESS MARY BOLKONSKAYA

Andrew's sister has a great deal in common with Sonya; perhaps this is what draws Nicholas to marry her. She is full of the notion of service to others. Patterned on Tolstoy's own mother, she is deeply spiritual, almost primitive in her faith. Marrying rather late, she nevertheless becomes an excellent mother.

PLATON KARATAEV

This peasant soldier, Pierre's companion in prison, is Tolstoy's major symbol of the good life. He exists, joyfully, from moment to moment sustained by the conviction that God exists, is good, is everywhere, and loves him. He is competent, energetic, takes the good and the bad without a care. Shot like a dog in the retreat by the retreating French, he dies as he had lived-with acceptance. Pierre's whole trouble existence is made suddenly meaningful by Platon's life and death.

TOLSTOY AND THE CRITICS

Almost from the date of its first publication *War and Peace* has been hailed as "the greatest novel ever written." From experts on the various battles there has been some criticism. Tolstoy answers these in "Some Words About *War and Peace*," published in the journal, *The Russian Achieves*, in 1868: "For an historian considering the achievement of a certain aim, there are heroes; for the artist treating of man's relation to all sides of life, there cannot and should not be heroes, but there should be men"; and again: "The historian has to deal with the results of the event, the artist with the fact of the event." To do this the artist must keep his eye on the probable, that is on how men probably act under such and such circumstances. Historians, depending on reports, and following these reports, only reconstruct an event. But often the reports are distorted or falsified. The artist can only follow the logic of his understanding of truth, of human character.

For the most part, however, this work has received universal praise. Tolstoy's influence on Thomas Mann, the great German novelist and Nobel Prize winner, on Marcel Proust, author of *Remembrance of Things Past*, and on Stephen Crane's *Red Badge of Courage* are merely examples of the mark he left on all future novelists. His techniques, some of which he developed from Dickens, Thackeray, and Stendhal, have proved fruitful. The way he introduces characters, his psychological comment, his ability to slip inside the character's imagination and allow the reader to know what the character is thinking, opened up the way for the many experiments of Henry James and James Joyce in interior monologue and point of view.

But in the last analysis, the general judgment of *War and Peace* is that no novel ever written has so vividly, completely, and with such verisimilitude and conviction recreated the illusion of life. William Lyon Phelps said of it that "it is a dictionary of life, where one may look up any passion, any ambition and find its meaning." Virginia Woolf said: "There is hardly any subject of human experience that is left out of *War and Peace.*" Perhaps the best comment on it is the one quoted from a lady by Aylmer Maude in a preface to his translation: "I should like to live my life over again, in order to have once again the pleasure of reading *War and Peace* for the first time."

THE RUSSIAN VIEW OF TOLSTOY

From the first, Russian critics realized they had a giant among them. Ivan Bunin (whom the student may recall as the author of "The Gentleman from San Francisco"), in his volume of reminiscences recalls Chekhov (father of the modern short story, author of *The Cherry Orchard*) saying that with Tolstoy towering over them they were all school children. With the coming of the Revolution of 1917 in Russia, Tolstoy did not suffer the same downgrading as did westernized Russians, such as Turgenev (Tolstoy's senior and the first of the Russian writers to influence the western world. Henry James, the great American novelist, regarded him as a master). Tolstoy's prescience about the coming revolt of the masses, his love of the peasants, his criticism of the government and of aristocratic society made him the hero of the Bolsheviks; he seemed in their eyes to be one of the prophets of the revolution. Aside from this, Tolstoy was a Russophile, that is, he rejected the Western values that Turgenev, for instance, prized so highly. He was convinced of the need to glorify the Russian people. In a sense, *War and Peace* is a great hymn of nationalism. More particularly, he shared with a whole group of Russians of his time, notably Dostoevsky, the belief in the "destiny" of the Russian people. In brief, this meant a belief in a special calling of the Russian people to save the world.

This kind of attitude, essentially religious, was translated by the Communists into secular terms, and this translation saved Tolstoy's reputation. Of course, distortions crept in. Tolstoy was regarded as anti-aristocratic in spite of the fact that he took special pains to make plain in his work his pride in being an aristocrat. His religious principles were regarded as aberrations. The great regard in which Tolstoy is held among the Soviets today is obvious when we consider the lavish production of the complete works to honor the author's centenary in 1928. This great edition makes available the total production of Tolstoy in ninety volumes. It is regarded as the supreme monument of Soviet scholarship.

TOLSTOY AND THE WESTERN WORLD

Curiously, Tolstoy has not been subjected to the same kind of close critical evaluation (which he deserves) that such authors as Joyce, Hemingway, Stendhal, and Camus have been given. This is the attitude which the world had towards Dickens until Edgar Johnson showed his complexity. In a sense, the greatest writers are so convincing, so true to life, so valid, that one takes them for granted. Shakespeare himself was taken for granted for some hundred and fifty years or more after his death. What is there, some feel, to be explained? It is all there and obvious. The one thing in Tolstoy that has attracted considerable attention, usually the attention of the raised eyebrow, is his view of history.

THE HEDGEHOG AND THE FOX

Isaiah Berlin has written perhaps the most important analysis of Tolstoy's view of history. At least, he takes it seriously. The reader will recall that Tolstoy's evaluation of the science of historicism is that it is no science. *War and Peace* is, in great measure, a demonstration of the only kind of valid history that can be written: man in particular places doing particular things

177

at particular times. Berlin analyzes this view of history, testing its validity, and though, on the whole, accepting its tenets as possibilities, he suggests that it may not be the whole story.

Philip Rahv, in *Images and Ideas* included two excellent essays on Tolstoy's art. The first of these, "The Green Twig and the Black Trunk," evaluates Tolstoy's art in terms of the flush of spring, intuition and insight against the enduring principles of **convention**, the elements which last from generation to generation, the new against the old, the moment against the enduring abstraction. This is an important and immensely readable essay.

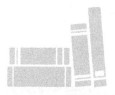

. . . .

Question: What is the **theme** of *War and Peace*?

Answer: The **theme** of *War and Peace* is nothing less than human existence itself, its rhythms, its interests, its hopes, ambitions, contradictions, satisfactions, pains. There is hardly a human emotion which is not explored, a possible human situation not included. On a vast and complex scale Tolstoy provides the reader with a representation of what life is; one cannot say that he has any specific and limited **theme**, such as "money," or "ambition," or "spiritual renewal," or "the terror of death" - typical unifying **themes** in many novels. If anything, his **theme** may be said to be "the search for identity" or "the search for the meaning of existence." He does not make a hobbyhorse even of this, however. In a sense he says to the reader: here in all its amazing vitality is what humanity is like; selfish, egotistical, and materialistic people are "bad" because they restrict humanity's development, unaggressive, forgiving, loving people are "good" because they contribute to humanity's development. The ultimate example of self-will is war and war is always vicious, never just, always evil, never to be excused. Boris' self-seeking and Napoleon's are different only in degree, not kind. Death comes to all. Man's duty is to realize that love alone can make man happy in this life.

Question: What is the relevance of the title *War and Peace*?

Answer: Tolstoy calls his novel *War and Peace* because these are the two extreme opposites of the human condition. Aside from being accurate to the contents of the narrative, it gives a clue to Tolstoy's technique in constructing the novel: events, emotions, episodes, characters, and settings are constantly played off against their opposites. Gaiety is opposed to despair, sadness to joy, family to society, spirituality to materialism, selfishness to humanitarianism. The examples pervade the entire novel: an obvious one is the entire narrative of Pierre matched against Andrew's. When Andrew is happy, Pierre is unhappy, and vice versa. Also we see Pierre married in turn to two women who have totally opposing characters: Helene, absolutely selfish, immoral, materialistic; Natasha, loving, moral, fine. But this is more than a structural device; it becomes a philosophic principle: life develops in rhythmic patterns, pulses up and down, meets resistance, dies or changes direction. Imagine Pierre's character if he had not married Helene, if he had not gone to Borodino. The accumulated acts of selfishness reaching a certain critical point boil off into a condition called war. But without that war would the Russian people have reached an awareness of their own identity? That is the paradox.

Question: In what categories can we usefully place Tolstoy's multitude of characters?

Answer: Although other classification systems can very well be devised (according to age, or sex, or social strata, or profession), one possible system is "good" and "bad" people. One cannot read very far in the novel without realizing that certain characters are presented in such a manner that we feel the author is sympathetic to them, others that he is unsympathetic to them. Insofar as this is so we have a clue as to which ways of life are desirable, which undesirable. The "good" people (Natasha, Andrew, Pierre, Nicholas, Sonya, Mary, and many others) are considerate, kind, they have depth and respond to situations. In a word, they grow. They test their principles, often find them inadequate or wrong, and attempt to change themselves. Others, the "bad" tend to be static and have no inner life. Dolokhov, the Karagin clan, Boris, Berg attempt to impose their wills on life, rather than let life change the direction of their wills. The "bad" are, in a sense, dead because they do not grow.

Question: What was Tolstoy's theory of history?

Answer: Tolstoy's theory of history is that a theory cannot be imposed upon it. It might be useful to go into some various ideas about history to make Tolstoy's negativism clearer. From the Greeks on, the generally accepted view of reality was that it was static and unchanging rather than dynamic and evolving. In other words, the fundamental elements of existence do not change. The past was, therefore, a model of how one should act or not act in the present. The historian's job was to clear past events of all accidental elements and present the essentials. Public men, especially "heroes," were the norms of action, for the simple reason that they were successful and memorable. With the rise of science, and science's demand that truth be based on empirical observation, certain historians, especially among the Germans, began to apply this same kind of exactness to historical studies. The historian must go to the records, all observations must be based on evidence, specific and concrete. The rest must necessarily be conjecture. It is against this Germanic, scientific emphasis on documents that Tolstoy rebels. He says documents may be distorted, they don't tell everything, they serve propagandistic ends. One can only be accurate as to what people might do in situations.

Question: What is Tolstoy's attitude toward the hero?

Answer: He denies that heroes exist, at least the way convention conceives of them. In this he takes a diametrically opposed position to that of Thomas Carlyle, the 19th century English historian and writer who promulgated the theory that history could best be understood in terms of its great men, it heroes (such as Napoleon) who rose up from time to time to direct humanity. It does not take more than a superficial reading of *War and Peace* to conclude that Tolstoy finds this a ridiculous point of view. Systematically he deprives Napoleon of all actual leadership in events; his successes were not due to his own will. Circumstances merely turned out well for him. All his vaunted genius for war and leadership can be explained by other means. Napoleon, riding the tip of a wave, imagined that he was directing the wave. Kutuzov was a true "hero," for the simple reason that he understood this. The only hero is he who directs the people to happiness and fruitful existence through the example of a selfless life. The rest is the vanity of egoism.

Question: What is the importance of suffering in Tolstoy?

Answer: Without suffering, according to Tolstoy, a human - among the ancient Hebrews and the classic Greeks; it is concepts of most religious. Without suffering one begins to feel secure, security leads to egoism, egoism leads to pride, pride a principle of Christian practice; it is found among the Preto inhumanity. In the novel all the "good" characters suffering cannot undergo moral regeneration. Suffering is an essential condition of the growth of the spirit. This attitude, of course, is not peculiar to Tolstoy; it is found everywhere for, and by their suffering attain spiritual growth. In the narratives of Andrew, Pierre, Mary, Natasha, note how their sufferings serve to make them question the values which they had once held valid. Note too that neither

Kuragin nor his children suffer, nor Boris, nor Napoleon. Success leads to their destruction. They never grow and never attain moral and spiritual maturity.

Question: *War and Peace* has been called "the perfect novel." Does it have any imperfections?

Answer: Overwhelmingly inclusive as Tolstoy's novel is, it does not of course include everything. In this sense it has imperfections. There are types of humanity who do not find a place in his gallery. There are for instance no notable portraits of intellectuals. Whenever Tolstoy treats a man of intellect he tends to do so ironically. In fact he distrusted systematic intellectualization, putting the heart and spirit over it. The Germans in the book are symbolic of the supremacy of mind over spirit. They are treated sarcastically.

There are other limitations. Because Tolstoy is committed to an epic sweep, the novel tends from time to time to become cluttered. It is difficult to see everything that is going on. Because of the need to cover a vast expanse of time, he cannot pause and explore situations in great depth. None of his characters deviate too greatly from the norm. We have no profound explorations of human conflict of a radical kind, as Dostoevsky gives us. Tolstoy's solution to the problems of existence tends to ignore personality differences. What works for Platon may not work in the same way for, say, Andrew. Tolstoy's constant emphasis on the principle of fatalism in human affairs tends to be annoying to the reader. What proof after all is there that if Napoleon had not existed the West would have invaded Russia? Yet his theory depends on the assumption that such would have been the case. One last thing: there are an inordinate number of situations in which the hand of the author is seen too obviously arranging the situation: of all the hundreds of places he could have been hospitalized, Andrew is conveniently situated with the Rostovs; before this, he finds himself being operated on next to his mortal enemy, Anatole Kuragin, also being operated on; Pierre is rescued by Dolokhov, his enemy; with the exactness of a seesaw Andrew's fortunes rise and fall while Pierre's fall and rise.

Question: How important is a knowledge of this period to an understanding of the setting of *War and Peace?*

Answer: From one point of view the answer to this is that knowledge of the period 1804 to 1812 is as unimportant as the knowledge of the period dealt with in the *Iliad* or the *Odyssey*. That is, these works all stand on their own. If they did not deal with material which has remained essentially timeless and enduring in themselves, they would not last. They are autonomous and self-contained. One can read and understand and love *War and Peace* for these self-contained and enduring qualities; its subject is after all human existence.

But human existence is never general. It has roots in particular people in particular times and places. For these reasons all the knowledge one can gain about Russia during the early part of the 19th Century will help us understand and appreciate the novel to a greater extent. For instance, the Russian aristocracy of the period felt that Russia was provincial and slightly barbaric. Hence they sought in French culture the values of civility and civilization they prized. They spoke French for the most part and practiced French fads and modes of behaviour. It is for this reason that they were divided in feelings about the French invaders. Another example is the attitude of Andrew and Pierre toward Napoleon. Both took a long time to cease regarding him as a great hero. The young people all over Europe held him in great esteem. At first he was regarded as a great spokesman for human freedom; later he was to be denounced as Europe's greatest threat to it.

Another example is the nature of the relationship of the serfs to the aristocrats in Russia of the period. How, one might say, can Count Rostov and Princess Mary be treated as good people when they had life and death rights over other human beings and could buy and sell them. Historical perspective is necessary here. One might recall that at the same period Washington and Jefferson owned slaves. Without justifying slavery, one can still see how certain social situations of long standing grow to be accepted even by those who are debased by them. One might recall the caste system in India, only recently eliminated legally, and the social structure of the Middle Ages throughout Europe. It is to Tolstoy's glory that he was one of the first to give freedom to his serfs and preach against it as an evil. It might be recalled, however, that the greatest difficulty Tolstoy encountered in freeing his serfs came from the serfs themselves, who thought he was trying to put something over on them.

Question: What is Tolstoy's doctrine of Art?

Answer: Tolstoy insisted that the function of art was **didactic**, that is, it should teach. Its purpose was not to entertain merely, nor to falsify life by sentimentality or melodrama. A corrupt man cannot be a true artist because his vision is off center. A corrupt man will produce corrupt art, and corrupt art will corrupt the people. What then should art teach? It should teach, over and over and over, the few enduringly valid principles of existence: Man must serve God and his fellowman; intellect is to be subjugated to heart and spirit; death will come to all; therefore, concentrate on the essentials, ignore material possessions, live as if this moment were the last, love everyone, destroy egoism and self-will. Demonstrations of what true art consists of may be found in Tolstoy's late short tales and stories, for example, "The Death of Ivan Ilych," How Much Land Does A Man Need?" and, especially, "God Sits in the Corner and Waits." It is interesting to note that after his spiritual struggles were over (when he was approximately fifty years old), Tolstoy repudiated the great masterpieces *War and Peace* and *Anna Karenina* as evil productions.

BIBLIOGRAPHY

CHIEF WRITINGS OF TOLSTOY

Tolstoy wrote constantly and voluminously throughout his long life. The complete Soviet edition of his works, published from 1928–1959, runs to ninety volumes. Most of these are not available in English. Of those available the student should be aware of the following: *The Cossacks* (1863), *War and Peace* (1865–1869), especially in the translation by Louise and Aylmer Maude, available in a Simon and Shuster edition published in 1958, *Anna Karenina* (1875–1877), *A Confession* (1879), *The Death of Ivan Ilych* (1886), *The Kreutzer Sonata* (1889), *What is Art?* (1897), *The Resurrection* (1899), *Hadjii Murad* (1896–1904).

Criticism

All told there is not a vast amount of criticism of Tolstoy in English. The student will find the following helpful: Matthew Arnold, "Count Leo Tolstoy," *Essays in Criticism*, Second Series (1888); Isaiah Berlin, *The Hedgehog and the Fox* (1953); Janks Lavin, *Tolstoy: An Approach* (1944); Thomas Mann, "Goethe and Tolstoy," *Essays of Three Decades* (1944); Philip Rahv, "Tolstoy: The Green Twig and Black Trunk," *Images and Ideas*, (1949); George Steiner, *Tolstoy or Dostoevsky* (1959); Stefan Zweig, *Adepts in Self Portraiture: Casanova, Stendhal, Tolstoy* (1952). R. F. Christian's *Tolstoy's "War and Peace": A Study* (1962) is the best available study of the novel's sources, its conception and development, its publication history, and its narrative and character techniques.

Biography

Leo Tolstoy by Ernest J. Simmons (1949) is considered to be the best and fullest biography of the author. In addition to Simmons' work on Tolstoy's life, the student will find these from one point of view or another: P. I. Birgukov, *The Life of Tolstoy* (1911); Derrick Leon, *Tolstoy: His Life and Work* (1944); Alymer Maude, *The Life of Tolstoy*, 2 vols. (1908–1810); Alexandra Tolstoy, *Tolstoy: A Life of My Father* (1953).